CYRANO DE BERGERAC

EDMOND ROSTAND was born in 1868 in Marseille. While studying law in Paris he pursued his literary interests (and his future wife, Rosemonde Gérard) in the salon of the poet Leconte de Lisle. Literature triumphed over the law: he published his first collection of poetry in 1890, and had a play performed at the Comédie-Française in 1894. Rostand then began to write roles for the *monstres sacrés* of *fin-de-siècle* Paris: *La Princesse lointaine* (1895) and *La Samaritaine* (1897) were both written for Sarah Bernhardt and enjoyed decent success. *Cyrano de Bergerac* (1897) was written for Coquelin *aîné*, the greatest French comic actor of the period; it enjoyed immediate and sensational acclaim. Rostand was created *chevalier de la Légion d'honneur* within only days of the first night, and elected to the Académie française in 1901. The remainder of his career was an anticlimax. His next play, *L'Aiglon* (1900), starring Sarah Bernhardt and Lucien Guitry, though successful, fell short of the triumph of *Cyrano de Bergerac*; increasingly afflicted by ill health, Rostand withdrew to his villa in the Pyrenees. It was ten years before he was able to complete another play, *Chantecler* (1910), an experimental drama which was poorly received. He died in Paris in 1918.

CHRISTOPHER FRY (b. 1907) rose to prominence in the late 1940s as a verse dramatist in the tradition of T. S. Eliot. He is especially remembered for the verbal exuberance of comedies like *The Lady's not for Burning* (1949) and *Venus Observed* (1950); he has also translated and adapted many French works for the English stage, including Anouilh's *Ring round the Moon* (1950) and *The Lark* (1955), and Giraudoux's *Tiger at the Gates* (1955) and *Duel of Angels* (1958). His version in rhyming — or 'chiming' — couplets of *Cyrano de Bergerac* was first performed at the 1975 Chichester Festival.

NICHOLAS CRONK is Fellow and Tutor in French at St Edmund Hall, Oxford. His previous publications include an edition of Voltaire's *Letters concerning the English Nation* (Oxford, 1994).

THE WORLD'S CLASSICS

EDMOND ROSTAND

Cyrano de Bergerac

A Heroic Comedy
in Five Acts

Translated by
CHRISTOPHER FRY

With an Introduction and Notes by
NICHOLAS CRONK

Oxford   New York
OXFORD UNIVERSITY PRESS
1996

Oxford University Press, Walton Street, Oxford OX2 6DP

Oxford New York

Athens Auckland Bangkok Bombay
Calcutta Cape Town Dar es Salaam Delhi
Florence Hong Kong Istanbul Karachi
Kuala Lumpur Madras Madrid Melbourne
Mexico City Nairobi Paris Singapore
Taipei Tokyo Toronto

and associated companies in
Berlin Ibadan

Oxford is a trade mark of Oxford University Press

First published as a World's Classics paperback 1996

British Library Cataloguing in Publication Data

Data available

Library of Congress Cataloging in Publication Data

Rostand, Edmond, 1868–1918.
[Cyrano de Bergerac. English]
Cyrano de Bergerac : a heroic comedy in five acts / Edmond Rostand ;
translated by Christopher Fry ; with an introduction and notes by
Nicholas Cronk.
p. cm. — (The world's classics)
Includes bibliographical references.
1. Cyrano de Bergerac, 1619–1655—Drama. 2. France—History—17th
century—Drama. 3. Authors, French—17th century—Drama. I. Fry,
Christopher. II. Cronk, Nicholas. III. Title. IV. Series.
PQ2635.O7C913 1996   842'.8—dc20   95–45197

ISBN 0–19–282424–4 (pbk.)

1 3 5 7 9 10 8 6 4 2

Typeset by Graphicraft Typesetters Ltd., Hong Kong
Printed in Great Britain by
BPC Paperbacks Ltd.
Aylesbury, Bucks.

CONTENTS

INTRODUCTION

Noses have a long and distinguished literary pedigree, from Pinocchio's prototype lie-detector to the nose in Gogol's story which breaks away from its owner and decides to lead a life of its own. Cyrano de Bergerac (1619–55) is, however, unusual among authors in being remembered almost uniquely for his nose. Thanks to Edmond Rostand (1868–1918), this seventeenth-century writer has become an emblem of *la vieille France*. Cyrano, as every Frenchman knows, had a great nose, he was a great lover (heterosexual, of course), and he was a great patriot. These three interestingly interconnected facts are all that are generally known about Cyrano, and they constitute such a powerfully held myth that it hardly matters that they are all entirely erroneous.

The 'real' Cyrano—perhaps one should say the 'other' Cyrano—was a writer of such dazzling unorthodoxy that he remains, even after three centuries, difficult to assess; indeed, his writings are still poorly known even in France. He was born and educated in Paris, but his life thereafter remains shrouded in mystery, and even in suspicion—an ideal foundation for the later growth of the legend. Cyrano embarked on a military career but it came to an abrupt end when he was badly wounded in the siege of Arras in 1640, and thereafter he seems to have devoted his life to writing. He was particularly associated with other burlesque writers like Scarron and Dassoucy, and he was, in both senses of the word—sexual and intellectual—a libertine. His reputation for debauchery was early established (he wrote a painfully graphic poem about his syphilis) and the tempestuous breakup of his homosexual affair with Dassoucy was much publicized. No less scandalous, however, and not entirely unconnected, was his attachment to the clandestine circle of atheistic free-thinkers then active in Paris; he was certainly influenced by the thought of the materialist philosopher Gassendi, whose pupil he may have been.

Cyrano's writing has an experimental and exploratory quality, and he essayed many genres: poetry, a tragedy, a comedy, and some spectacularly vitriolic political pamphlets against Mazarin. The 1640s and 1650s were turbulent years in France: politically, because the increasingly powerful monarchy had not yet imposed its centralizing will, and philosophically because under the impact of the 'scientific revolution' philosophers like Descartes and scientists like Galileo were beginning to question fundamentally the orthodox world-view. In this climate, Cyrano thrived as a radical and controversial figure; when he died after being hit on the head by a falling beam, it was only to be expected that there would be gossip about a plot. His most enduring work is a satirical novel, first published (heavily expurgated) in 1657, *L'Autre Monde* (*The Other World*, also known as *Voyages to the Moon and the Sun*); a pioneering work of science fiction, this burlesque philosophical novel imagines a moon world in which all earthly assumptions—scientific, religious, linguistic, sexual—are comically turned topsy-turvy and so cast into doubt. Cyrano is scornful of tradition and authority, and in applying his robust rationalism to Christianity and to Aristotelian philosophy and science, he anticipates thinkers of the French Enlightenment like Voltaire and Diderot. But, as often happens with radically subversive writers, Cyrano was marginalized as an eccentric. Thus the 'real' Cyrano was forgotten soon after his death, and he remained forgotten until the mid-nineteenth century.

The legendary Cyrano burst onto the scene with newly invented panache in 1897 when Edmond Rostand's 'heroic comedy' *Cyrano de Bergerac* received its première to huge acclaim. What made an up-and-coming dramatist choose to write a play about a seemingly obscure seventeenth-century literary figure? The revival of Cyrano de Bergerac's literary reputation had in fact begun already in the middle years of the century. In reaction against what they saw as the excessively rule-bound literature of French Classicism dating from the period of Louis XIV's absolute rule (1661–1715), certain Romantic writers in the 1830s and 1840s revived interest in the less conventional writers who had flourished in the 'pre-classical' (and 'pre-absolutist') period. Charles Nodier and Théophile Gautier both wrote enthusiastically about Cyrano, and in particular it was the poet Gautier who, in an influential essay in *Les Grotesques* (1844), invented the myth of Cyrano's long nose. An edition of Cyrano's writings published in 1858 made his work easily available to the public for the first time since the seventeenth century. Furthermore the reprinting in that edition of a seventeenth-century account of Cyrano's career by his friend Le Bret gave new life to many old inaccuracies, including the false notion that Cyrano came from Bergerac in Gascony, in the south-west of France (where today there is a brisk tourist trade in postcards of Cyrano). In fact, the 'Bergerac' of his name is a small town near Paris, as was shown in a thesis on Cyrano's life and works presented at the Sorbonne in 1893 by Pierre Brun; Rostand seems not to have used Brun's work in writing his play, and anyway it suited his purposes to present Cyrano as a southerner.

Edmond Rostand, unlike Cyrano, really was from the South of France. Born in Marseille, he went to Paris to complete his education, and it was in the capital that he began in the 1890s to make a name for himself as a dramatist and poet. The première of *Cyrano* at the Théâtre de la Porte-Saint-Martin in Paris on 28 December 1897 was a sensational success which has become part of French theatrical legend. It transformed Rostand, overnight, into the leading French literary celebrity of the day; within two months of the first night, Toulouse-Lautrec had produced a lithograph of Coquelin *aîné* in the role of Cyrano. Coquelin and Sarah Bernhardt performed the play in New York in 1900, and the following year in London (though Bernhardt never performed the role of Roxane in France). And in 1901, when still only in his early thirties, Rostand was elected to the Académie française. He went on to write several other works for the stage, notably *L'Aiglon*, and *Chantecler*, which is sometimes considered his best work. But he was never able to repeat the popular success of *Cyrano*. When Rostand died, just three weeks after the end of the First World War, it was for *Cyrano* that he was remembered. The early reception of the play was phenomenal: it reached its thousandth Paris performance in 1913, and it has been estimated that in that one year alone there were altogether 3,000 performances in France.

No other French play in the period enjoyed anything like this success with the public: *Cyrano* evidently touched a chord in the audience of the time, and to understand the play's unprecedented impact we need to look more closely at the state of France in the 1880s and 1890s, the period which the French themselves dubbed the *fin-de-siècle*. France achieved national unity far later than is generally supposed, and the need to forge a national identity was still keenly felt at the turn of the century:

Despite evidence to the contrary, inhabitants of the hexagon in 1870 generally knew themselves to be French subjects, but to many this status was no more than an abstraction. The people of whole regions felt little identity with the state or with people of other regions. Before this changed, before the inhabitants of France could come to feel a significant community, they had to share significant experiences with each other. Roads, railroads, schools, markets, military service, and the circulation of money, goods, and printed matter provided those experiences, swept away old commitments, instilled a national view of things in regional minds, and confirmed the power of that view by offering advancement to those who adopted it. The national ideology was still diffuse and amorphous around the middle of the nineteenth century. French culture became truly national only in the last years of the century.[1]

Cyrano is certainly a celebration of France and of Frenchness; and the symbolism is all the more powerful because Cyrano is depicted as a Gascon, a southerner, fighting for the glory of the French nation as a whole. Cyrano and his fellow soldiers are suspicious of the power and pretensions of the Comte de Guiche: but when in Act IV the Comte's accent slips and he reveals himself as a man of the Midi, all are reconciled.

Another feature of the *fin-de-siècle* is bewilderment at the speed of change. Charles Péguy, a poet of peasant stock, wrote in *L'Argent* (1913) that the world had changed more since his school-days in

---

[1] Eugen Weber, *Peasants into Frenchmen: The Modernization of Rural France, 1870–1914* (London, 1977), 486.

the 1880s than it had changed from the time of the Romans to the 1880s. The telegraph, the telephone, the typewriter, the electric light, the lift, the bicycle, the tram, the Métro are all innovations of the *fin-de-siècle*, and some, like the bicycle, were advertised in the vivacious and highly coloured posters which are so characteristic of Paris at this time. Yet notwithstanding the real improvement in living standards experienced by large parts of the population, the *fin-de-siècle* saw itself as a period of moral and artistic decadence. The material progress constituted by these new inventions 'may have helped palliate the shortcomings of the political class,' writes Eugen Weber, 'but they disturbed the more austere who feared for the national fibre'.[2]

Cyrano's swashbuckling courage and ticklish sense of honour might seem out of place in this world of typewriters and bicycles; but the aristocratic ethos of personal honour survived with surprising persistence in the bourgeoisie of the Third Republic—it has been estimated that there were as many as 300 duels a year in France in the 1880s and 1890s, many of them involving journalists, writers, and politicians. Cyrano's penchant for flamboyant duelling takes on a new colouring when we recall that the Radical politician Georges Clemenceau, nicknamed 'the Tiger', fought twenty-two duels in his career, all of them widely reported in the press; a restaurant on the Grande Jatte outside Paris was a favoured rendezvous of duellists, and its owner claimed that Clemenceau booked an average of three duels a week. So when de Guiche tells the Gascon cadets fighting for France at the siege of Arras 'You are all unrivalled in courage', he speaks directly to the concerns of the *fin-de-siècle*:

In the context of military crisis and fear of national decline that reigned in France in the period 1890–1914, courage was a universally prized quality . . . Because the French lagged behind Germany in both material resources and population, they were obliged to compensate for this deficit by developing superior 'spiritual' qualities, of which courage was perhaps the most important . . . One is able to find considerable evidence of a self-conscious

[2] Eugen Weber, *France, Fin de Siècle* (Cambridge, Mass., 1986), 4.

social effort to cultivate the noble flowers of courage and heroism and eradicate the weeds of cowardice and fear that inhibited their growth.[3]

The Third Republic could never forget that it had come into being with the Prussian invasion of France in 1870, and although by the 1890s the Republic seemed to be established, the political scene was none the less turbulent. Memories of the humiliation of the Franco-Prussian War were still keen—when *Lohengrin* was performed in Paris in 1891 (the first Wagner production by the Opéra since 1861), the police had to be called in to quell the riots. In the years 1887–9, General Boulanger and his supporters had come close to overthrowing the Republic, and the Panama scandal of 1892, a financial scandal which affected prominent politicans including Clemenceau, provoked further unrest. The Socialist movement was growing, and in the years 1892–4 there were a series of anarchist explosions in Paris; then in 1894 President Carnot was stabbed to death in Lyon by an Italian anarchist. The anarchist movement made a deep impression on French culture in the 1890s, affecting literature and the visual arts as much as politics.[4] The Republic appeared to have lost its way, and a succession of moderate governments struggled in vain to calm the crisis.

It was against this background of instability that the Dreyfus Affair erupted. In 1894, Captain Alfred Dreyfus, a Jewish army officer, was found guilty of spying for the Germans, and sentenced to deportation to Devil's Island; new evidence subsequently invalidated the court martial's verdict, but the army, supported by the government, sought to suppress it. The existence of this evidence became publicly known in late 1897, so that the Affair had reached a point of crisis just at the moment of the première of *Cyrano*. Less than a fortnight after the triumphant first night, on 10 January 1898, Major Esterhazy, the true spy, was acquitted by a court martial, prompting Émile Zola, three days later, to publish his article

[3] Robert A. Nye, *Masculinity and Male Codes of Honor in Modern France* (New York, 1993), 217–18.
[4] See Richard D. Sonn, *Anarchism and Cultural Politics in Fin de Siècle France* (Lincoln, Nebr., 1989).

'*J'Accuse*', an open letter to the President, Félix Faure (who only a week earlier had attended with his family a performance of *Cyrano*). 'From Zola's manifesto,' writes John McManners, 'France was riven by a moral cataclysm.'[5] The nation was split into two warring camps, the *Dreyfusards*, who demanded a retrial for Dreyfus, and the anti-*Dreyfusards*, who stood by the original verdict, and who, against all the evidence, supported Army and Church. This became the defining issue dividing Left and Right, creating a split which brought to a head all manner of tensions in the Third Republic: monarchist versus republican, Catholic versus Protestant/Jew/Freemason, army versus anti-militarist. It was to have long-lasting political repercussions, most notably the legal separation of Church and State in 1905; in the short term, the Republic was further destabilized, and when President Faure died in 1899 (not at the hands of an anarchist but in the arms of his mistress), his funeral became the occasion for an attempted *coup d'état* which farcically demonstrated the fragility of the regime.

The leading authors of the day were prominent in these political debates, and indeed the Affair played a pivotal role in defining the modern French notion of the literary intellectual; Zola, Proust, and Anatole France were among the *Dreyfusards*, while the opposing camp included Claudel and Valéry. Rostand was also a *Dreyfusard* but, like Gide (who was a year his junior), he did not adopt a high profile in the Affair, and his sympathy for the cause of Dreyfus does not appear to have alienated his potential audience—on the contrary, the extraordinary reception given to the play suggests that *Cyrano* appealed to audiences across the divide opened up by the Dreyfus Affair. In a political atmosphere which was so tense, every detail of the play could be politically charged (and not least, in this climate of rabid anti-Semitism, the possession of an oversize nose). On the one hand, the play offers us the comforting image of a brave and fearless soldier who hails from a golden age of French military might; on the other hand, Cyrano is an anti-establishment figure, fiercely independent, who relishes challenging authority.

---

[5] John McManners, *Church and State in France, 1870–1914* (London, 1972), 118.

One explanation for the phenomenal early success of *Cyrano* is that it spoke to all Frenchmen and united them as few other works of the period could have done.

If this was a time of political turbulence, it was a period of artistic challenge too, the era of Symbolism and *fin-de-siècle* Decadence, when the avant-garde was provoking a powerful conservative backlash. It was only in February 1897, for example, after a prolonged battle, that the first Impressionist paintings were publicly displayed, in the musée du Luxembourg. Of all the art forms, it was theatre which, in Paris at least, was the most popular and the most diverse. A journalist of the time observed that 'the population of Paris lives in the theatre, for the theatre, by the theatre', and it has been estimated that in the 1880s and 1890s half a million Parisians visited the theatre once a week, and more than twice that number once a month.[6]

The plays that they flocked to see were not, by and large, the plays dwelt on at length in the literary histories. Alfred Jarry's *Ubu-Roi* (1896) played for just one performance, and Maurice Maeterlinck's *Pelléas et Mélisande* (1892) is remembered now largely on account of Debussy's opera (1902). While the Paris premières of Ibsen, Strindberg, and Hauptmann played for short runs in small theatres (not always with success—during performances of Ibsen's *Wild Duck*, sections of the public took to quacking at inopportune moments), the masses flocked to see highly spectacular productions of melodramas, fairy-tales, and adventure stories. Rostand's great achievement with *Cyrano* was to write a play which defied easy categorization, a drama which was neither modern nor traditional, and yet both at the same time. The seventeenth-century setting evokes the period of France's military and political supremacy; yet this vision of the Age of Richelieu also evokes an earlier nineteenth-century treatment of the period, Dumas's *The Three Musketeers* (1844)—it is a nice touch that d'Artagnan should meet Cyrano fleetingly in the first act.

Rostand's choice of subject remains, however, a surprising one.

---

[6] Weber, *France, Fin de Siècle*, 159.

Introduction

It was during the last years of the century that literary history was 'invented' as a scientific discipline, as exemplified in Gustave Lanson's monumental *Histoire de la littérature française* (1895). The school and university syllabuses of the Third Republic, influenced by the new literary histories, gave canonical status to seventeenth-century French Classicism. Lanson's seventeenth century is the Age of the Sun King, an era of religious and political orthodoxy; the free-thinking, distinctly unorthodox Cyrano de Bergerac hardly fits into this view of the *grand siècle*, so Lanson's *Histoire* consigns him to a footnote. It is a pleasing paradox, and a tribute to Rostand's knowledge of the seventeenth century, that his wilfully inaccurate and anachronistic play did more to restore the literary fortunes of Cyrano de Bergerac than all the positivistic literary criticism of the Sorbonne professors.

Written in five acts and in alexandrine (twelve-syllable) rhyming couplets, Rostand's play mimics the form of seventeenth-century classical theatre, an example of which he incorporates into the opening act (in imitation of Molière's *L'Impromptu de Versailles*); but again, the classicism is more apparent than real. Rostand did not repeat the mistake made by the librettists of Massenet's opera *Le Cid* (1885), Édouard Blau and Louis Gallet, who incorporated into their libretto lines lifted directly from Corneille's drama; this attempt at authenticity produced only oddness, partly because alexandrines are difficult to set to music, but partly also because a poetic language ripped from its context loses its dramatic cogency. Rostand well understood one of the key principles of French classical poetics, that what is plausible (*vraisemblable*) matters more than what is true (*vrai*): his alexandrines sound authentic precisely because they are not. A parallel may be found in the most characteristic artistic expression of these years, *Art Nouveau*. This style, though unquestionably new, was explicitly inspired by the principles of the rococo; it was a means by which the grace and elegance of the Louis XV interior could be recreated in the decade following the construction

[7] See Debora L. Silverman, *Art Nouveau in Fin-de-Siècle France: Politics, Psychology, and Style* (Berkeley, 1989).

[xv]

of the Eiffel Tower (1889).[7] Rostand, for his part, creates a dramatic *Art Nouveau*, evoking an older style with all its connotations of tradition and charm, while in fact creating something entirely original.

In fact Rostand's understanding of drama owes more to Romanticism than to Classicism; Cyrano, for example, has a more than passing resemblance to Don César de Bazan, a noble poet, in Hugo's *Ruy Blas* (1838), a verse drama set in seventeenth-century Spain. (In writing the role of Cyrano for Coquelin, Rostand was surely influenced by the fact that Don César had been one of Coquelin's great parts.) It was Hugo, in his *Préface de Cromwell* (1827), who made the most influential contribution to Romantic aesthetics, arguing that classical tragedy should be replaced by a new form of drama which could combine the contrasting elements of the beautiful and the ugly, the comic and the tragic, the 'grotesque' and the 'sublime'. Victor Hugo's dramas have mainly survived in operatic form: Verdi's *Rigoletto*, based on Hugo's *Le Roi s'amuse*, is a notable example of the sublime–grotesque combination. The character of Cyrano is the perfect exemplar of this Romantic dichotomy, sublime in his courage and his unrequited love, and grotesque in his appearance. Hugo's precise terms are put into the mouth of Roxane in Act IV: she is so in love with Christian that 'nothing could make him grotesque to me!' (p. 124); and after learning of his death, there is more dramatic irony when she tells Cyrano that Christian possessed 'a sublime mind' (p. 126).

Cyrano has been seen in this perspective as the last great Romantic drama in the tradition of Victor Hugo; if so, it is the only one to have found a permanent place in the repertoire. But a Romantic drama played out against the backcloth of *fin-de-siècle* Decadence cannot be the same as a Romantic drama played in the context of the Restoration or the July Monarchy; if it is true that the Romantics were fighting a rearguard action 'against the new scientific rationalism',[8] by the time of Rostand's generation the fight had been lost, and positivism had triumphed. To hark back

---

[8] George Steiner, *The Death of Tragedy* (London, 1963), 198.

to the days of Romanticism was a deliberate anachronism and of course a major part of the play's appeal for its early audiences. But this is more than mere nostalgia or escapism. What is most remarkable about the work—and what distinguishes it from true Romantic drama—is its self-conscious and bravura use of parody and pastiche. The play is nothing less than a patchwork anthology of French literary history, and it flatters and amuses its audience by assuming familiarity with the French literary tradition.

The power of pastiche is demonstrated to good effect in Cyrano's death scene. In a moment of great pathos, Cyrano includes in his fictional gazette to Roxane the news of his own death; the emotion of the scene is complicated by the fact that it recalls the final scene of Zola's recently published *Le Docteur Pascal* (1893), whose protagonist is a rationalist engaged in a struggle against religious prejudice. Then, as his final moment approaches, Cyrano rises from his chair, to die beneath a tree, in precise imitation of the hero of the *Chanson de Roland*. Within one short scene Rostand moves effortlessly from an allusion to a Naturalist novel to pastiche of a medieval epic.

This dense literary allusiveness gives depth and complexity to the character of Cyrano. When, in Act II, Cyrano is asked by the comte de Guiche if he has read *Don Quixote*, he replies:

> With great delight.
> I take my hat off to that old fly-by-night. (p. 55)

No nineteenth-century spectator could have failed to appreciate the playfulness of this remark. Cervantes's novel was widely known in nineteenth-century France, and it had been the subject of numerous plays, including one by Victorien Sardou, revived with music in 1895; Don Quixote, in the wake of Romanticism, was seen to exemplify the hero who was simultaneously sublime and grotesque. The quixotic hero, ridiculous but idealistic, saintly but farcical, became something of a nineteenth-century type, and Cervantes's comic protagonist is father to some unexpected offspring, among them Captain Ahab in Melville's *Moby-Dick* (1851), the hero of

Dostoevsky's *The Idiot* (1868), Maxi in Galdós's *Fortunata y Jacinta* (1887)—and Rostand's Cyrano de Bergerac.[9]

Other dramatists tried to imitate the formula of *Cyrano*, but without success. It is wholly appropriate that the one theatrical work inspired by *Cyrano* which continues to hold the stage is (ostensibly) based on *Don Quixote*: the opera *Don Quichotte*, by Massenet, premièred at Monte Carlo in 1910. The librettist of this work, Henri Cain, used the same designation, 'comédie héroïque', which Rostand had used to describe his play, and the conception of the title role (written for Chaliapin) owes more to Rostand than to Cervantes: this is a Cyranesque version of Don Quixote, noble and idealistic, funny yet touching, unlucky in love and brave in battle. There are specific borrowings, too: Quichotte, like Cyrano, works out the rhymes of a poem in mid-duel; and both protagonists die a hero's death beneath a tree. Massenet—a witness at Rostand's marriage—was the other towering figure of Parisian theatre at this time, and the considerable success of his late opera a tribute to the continuing popularity of Rostand's play during the *Belle Époque*.

Cyrano de Bergerac enjoyed instant and phenomenal fame, so it is all the more astonishing that the popularity of the play has endured. It continues to please audiences, in defiance of fashion, and rather to the annoyance of authors and critics who have sometimes treated the work with condescension—'Claudel or Rostand,' said Gide, 'you have to choose.' In France the play has been constantly performed; after Rostand's death, there were revivals in 1928, 1929, and 1936; in 1938 the work received ultimate recognition by being taken into the repertoire of the Comédie-Française, where it received 415 performances in the period 1938–53. The central role, like that of Dumas's Kean, has provided a challenge for every great French actor, among them Pierre Fresnay (1928), Pierre Dux (1956), Jacques Charon (1964, at the Comédie-Française); Jacques Weber (1983), and Jean-Paul Belmondo (1990). There have been

[9] See Anthony Close, *The Romantic Approach to Don Quixote* (Cambridge, 1978), 54.

numerous films based on the play, from an Italian silent film of 1909 to, most recently, the immensely successful film of Jean-Paul Rappeneau (1990), starring Gérard Depardieu as Cyrano. Recent English actors to have tackled the role of Cyrano include Keith Michell (Chichester, 1975), in the present translation by Christopher Fry; Derek Jacobi (RSC, 1983), in Anthony Burgess's translation; and Robert Lindsay (Haymarket, 1992), in a translation by John Wells. The poet Edwin Morgan demonstrated the play's versatility by devising a version in broad Glaswegian (Edinburgh Festival, 1992). The Indian film star Naseeruddin Shah played Cyrano in a production set in 1930s India, adapted by Jatinder Verma, and translated by Ranjit Bolt (Royal National Theatre, 1995). Irek Mukhamedov danced the title role in a three-act ballet *Cyrano* staged by the Royal Ballet and choreographed by David Bintley (Covent Garden, 1991).

How are we to explain the remarkable staying power, and stage power, of this 'heroic comedy'? In the first place, this is a play which is self-consciously theatrical, about a character who is a consummate actor: no wonder that every great actor has wanted to play the role. The action begins in a theatre where we are invited to mock a famous actor for his stilted and inflated manner of delivery; Cyrano outperforms Montfleury in an improvisation which demonstrates his own superiority as an actor; he acts when he is with Christian to conceal his love, and he also acts with Christian to help his young friend express his love; he acts with and for the cadets when they are weary with hunger; and he goes on acting with Roxane, long after Christian's death; when she finally sees through his performance, the play must end.

The crucial feature of Cyrano's self-aware performance is that it is in verse—*Cyrano* in prose would be unthinkable. Cyrano is a poet as much as he is an actor. His poetry is often distinctively Baroque, as in his Act I tirade on noses (which recalls certain early seventeenth-century French poems), but the poetry always has theatrical purpose. Cyrano provokes his antagonist in Act I not so much by fighting him as by composing a ballad as he does so; he soothes the cadets in Act IV by capping their complaints: 'Always the clever phrase!' remarks one of their number, to which Cyrano replies,

> Why, yes, the phrase,
> The point driven home!—The way I would choose to die
> Would be at evening under a glowing sky,
> Saying a good thing in a good cause! (p. 99)

Roxane is seduced less by Christian's beauty than by Cyrano's poetry, and it is because of his letters that she risks everything to visit him; it is Cyrano's poetic voice which finally gives him away in the final act. Cyrano is a Romantic hero in his use of poetry to express feeling, and a Baroque hero in his wielding of language to make an effect: thus the actor and the poet coalesce.

Verse drama is not now much in fashion, either in France or in England (though Caryl Churchill's *Serious Money* had a highly successful run in London in 1987). Nor was it in fashion in France in the 1890s, when the tendency toward realism in theatre militated against drama in prose; Rostand, who wrote only verse drama, cut a singular figure. In England, Christopher Fry is the most recent playwright to have made verse his natural mode of dramatic expression, hence his verbally dazzling translation of *Cyrano*. Writing the year after Rostand's death, T. S. Eliot evoked 'the disappearance of the poet, whom, more than any other in France, we treated as the exponent of "rhetoric", thinking of rhetoric as something recently out of fashion'. He goes on to describe how the poetic rhetoric of Cyrano is an intrinsic part of his dramatic identity:

Is not Cyrano exactly in this position of contemplating himself as a romantic, a dramatic figure? This dramatic sense on the part of the characters themselves is rare in modern drama. In sentimental drama it appears in a degraded form, when we are evidently intended to accept the character's sentimental interpretation of himself. In plays of realism we often find parts which are never allowed to be consciously dramatic, for fear, perhaps, of their appearing less real. But in actual life, in many of those situations in actual life which we enjoy consciously and keenly, we are at times aware of ourselves in this way, and these moments are of very great usefulness to dramatic verse. A very small part of acting is that which takes place on the stage! Rostand had—whether he had anything else or not—this dramatic sense, and it is what gives life to Cyrano. It is a sense which is almost a sense of humour (for when anyone is conscious of himself as acting, something like a sense of humour is present). It gives Rostand's characters—Cyrano at least—a gusto which is uncommon on the modern stage. No doubt Rostand's people play up to this too steadily. We recognize that in the love scenes of Cyrano in the garden, for in *Romeo and Juliet* the profounder dramatist shows his lovers melting into unconsciousness of their isolated selves, shows the human soul in the process of forgetting itself. Rostand could not do that; but in the particular case of Cyrano on Noses, the character, the situation, the occasion were perfectly suited and combined. The tirade generated by this combination is not only genuinely and highly dramatic: it is possibly poetry also.[10]

The moral force of this poetry can be summed up in one word, a word which Rostand invents for the purpose: *panache*. It is also a word which Rostand has given to the English language. In its primary sense, it refers to the plume of feathers on a helmet, but its figurative sense of 'display, swagger, verve' is first attested in English in 1898, in the first English translation of *Cyrano*. (The word quickly caught on: G. B. Shaw uses it in *Man and Superman* in 1903.) In French, the figurative use of 'panache' predates Rostand, but only just, and it is Rostand who establishes definitively its modern sense.[11] He was clearly proud of having fathered the term; when in March 1898 he addressed the pupils of the Collège Stanislas, his former school, he urged them to turn their faces against modern cynicism and to hold fast to the military ethos of a former age: 'Empanachez-vous donc'.

Five years later Rostand took his seat at the Académie française, and in his traditional *discours de réception*, he proposed to his fellow academicians a definition of panache:

To joke in the face of danger is the supreme politeness, a delicate refusal to cast oneself as a tragic hero; panache is therefore a timid heroism, like the smile with which one excuses one's superiority. Heroes lacking panache

---

[10] T. S. Eliot, ' "Rhetoric" and Poetic Drama', in *Selected Essays* (London, 1951), 40–1.

[11] According to the *Trésor de la langue française*, the first attested use of 'panache' in its figurative sense is by Sainte-Beuve in 1854. It also occurs in Zola's novel *Rome* (1896); this usage only becomes frequent, however, after *Cyrano de Bergerac*.

are certainly more disinterested than others, since, in making a sacrifice, panache often brings with it an attitude of consolation. A little frivolous perhaps, most certainly a little theatrical, panache is nothing but a grace; but a grace which is so difficult to retain in the face of death, a grace which demands so much strength that, all the same, it is a grace . . . which I wish for all of us.

For a variety of reasons—political, economic, social, cultural—French society of the *fin-de-siècle* found itself divided, unconfident, and anxious. 'Modern society', wrote Zola in 1896, 'is endlessly racked by a nervous irritability. We are sick and tired of progress, industry, and science.' Looking back in 1913, Rostand admitted in an interview that this mood had encouraged him to write his play:

It was a strange period. The leading lights of the moment were Ibsen, Émile Zola. It was the time of realism, naturalism, scepticism . . . How many writers, playwrights who were then busy pushing this naturalism and this scepticism are now formidable proponents of traditional values, of—*mon Dieu*, let's use the word, the word which came into fashion as a result of *Cyrano*—of 'panache'! . . . I wrote *Cyrano* for pleasure, happily and with love, and also, I admit it, with the idea of fighting against the tendencies of the time. Tendencies which, to be truthful, infuriated me and revolted me.[12]

Panache is Rostand's answer to the ills and anxieties of modernity. Nearly a century later, in another *fin-de-siècle*, the anxieties remain as compelling, and the attraction of panache still as potent. At the same time, panache embodies an ethic which confirms for the French their own favourite image of themselves, as gallant, romantic, intrepid, even to the point of extravagance. This, above all, is the reason why the play retains its power over modern audiences. A journalist writing in *Le Figaro* in 1976 put it more simply: 'Cyrano, c'est la France.'

[12] *Les Annales*, 9 Mar. 1913.

SELECT BIBLIOGRAPHY

There is a study of the play in English by E. Freeman, *Rostand: 'Cyrano de Bergerac'*, in the series *Glasgow Introductory Guides to French Literature* (Glasgow, 1995). The only general work on Rostand available in English is Alba Amoia's *Edmond Rostand* (Boston, 1978). T. S. Eliot discusses *Cyrano de Bergerac* in his essay ' "Rhetoric" and Poetic Drama' (1919), included in his *Selected Essays* (London, 1951). The following essays are also of interest: W. D. Howarth, '*Cyrano de Bergerac*, or the Triumph of Romantic Drama', in *Sublime and Grotesque: A Study of French Romantic Drama* (London, 1975), 386–98; and Patricia Elliott Williams, 'Some Classical Aspects of *Cyrano de Bergerac*', *Nineteenth-Century French Studies*, 1 (1973), 112–24.

For readers of French, there is an edition of the French text, with notes and an introduction in English, by Geoff Woollen (Bristol, 1994). The authoritative critical edition of the text is that of Jacques Truchet (Paris, 1983); this contains a full bibliography. The best account of Rostand's life is that of Émile Ripert, *Edmond Rostand* (1930; republished Paris, 1968). The following critical studies are particularly recommended: Paul Vernois, 'Architecture et écriture théâtrale dans *Cyrano de Bergerac*', *Travaux de linguistique et de littérature*, 4/2 (1966), 111–38; and André Blanchard, 'Edmond Rostand, Cyrano et la poésie baroque ou précieuse', *Points et contrepoints*, 109 (Dec. 1973), 29–34.

The best introduction to the seventeenth-century author Cyrano de Bergerac is his novel *L'Autre Monde ou les estats et empires de la lune*; there is a good edition by Madeleine Alcover (Paris, 1977), and an English translation by Richard Aldington, *Voyages to the Moon and the Sun* (London, 1991).

Select Bibliography

The film of Jean-Paul Rappeneau (1990), starring Gérard Depardieu, is available on video, with English subtitles by Anthony Burgess (London: Artificial Eye, 1992).

A CHRONOLOGY OF
EDMOND ROSTAND

1868 (1 April) Rostand born in Marseille.

1878 Begins studies at the lycée of Marseille.

1884 Continues studies in Paris, at the Collège Stanislas.

1887 Receives a prize from the Académie de Marseille for his essay 'Deux romanciers de Provence: Honoré d'Urfé et Émile Zola'.

1889 *Le Gant rouge* is performed, without success.

1890 Publishes his first collection of verse, *Les Musardises*, which is well received by the critics. Marries the poet Rosemonde Gérard.

1891 *Les Deux Pierrots* is refused by the Comédie-Française.

1894 *Les Romanesques* is performed at the Comédie-Française.

1895 Première of *La Princesse lointaine*, with Sarah Bernhardt and Lucien Guitry. The famous actor Constant-Benoît Coquelin, known as Coquelin *aîné*, asks Rostand for a play: it will be *Cyrano de Bergerac*.

1896 In the Dreyfus Affair which is traumatizing France, declares himself a *Dreyfusard*.

1897 (April) Première of *La Samaritaine*, again with Sarah Bernhardt.

(Dec.) *Cyrano* given its first performance at the Théâtre de la Porte-Saint-Martin. The first night is a sensation, and the work plays for 400 performances until March 1899. Until his death in Jan. 1909, Coquelin is the only actor to play the lead role in Paris, where there are revivals at the Porte-Saint-Martin (1900, 1902, 1903); then, with new sets, at the Théâtre de la Gaîté (annually from 1904 to the beginning of 1907); then again at the Porte-Saint-Martin from 1907 until Dec. 1908.

1898 (1 Jan.) Created *chevalier de la Légion d'honneur*.

(6 Jan.) President Félix Faure attends with his family a performance of *Cyrano*.

Rostand elected to the Académie des sciences morales et politiques. *Cyrano* tours the French provinces, beginning, in March, in Marseille, Rostand's home town. The play is also performed in Berlin and London. Two English translations are published (one in London, one in New York), and 'panache' (in the sense of 'swagger') enters the English language.

1900 Première of *L'Aiglon*, with Sarah Bernhardt and Lucien Guitry. Rostand settles at Cambo-les-Bains in the Pyrenees, on account of ill health.

1901 Elected to the Académie française, at the very early age of 33, and created *officier de la Légion d'honneur*. Coquelin and Sarah Bernhardt perform *Cyrano* in London.

1904 With his earnings from *Cyrano*, begins to build near Cambo-les-Bains a large house in the Basque style, 'Arnaga' (since 1963 the Musée Edmond Rostand), where he will spend the rest of his life.

1910 Première, poorly received, of *Chantecler*, with Lucien Guitry. Rostand is created *commandeur de la Légion d'honneur*.

1913 *Cyrano* is revived with new sets at the Théâtre de la Porte-Saint-Martin, with Charles Le Bargy in the lead role. The work reaches its thousandth performance in Paris; and soon after, in celebration, there is a free public performance.

1918 (2 Dec.) Rostand dies in Paris, six weeks after the Armistice, a victim of Spanish flu.

1919 Publication of *Le Vol de la Marseillaise*, a collection of poetry written during the War.

1921 Publication of Rostand's last play, *La Dernière Nuit de Don Juan*, first performed in 1922.

1983 *Cyrano* enters the public domain; the number of performances to date is estimated at over 14,000.

Cyrano drawn by Edmond Rostand

CYRANO DE BERGERAC

A Heroic Comedy in Five Acts

It was to the soul of CYRANO that I intended to dedicate this poem.

But since his soul has been reborn in you, COQUELIN,* I dedicate it to you.

E. R.

ACT ONE

The Hall of the Hôtel de Bourgogne in 1640. At the rising of the curtain the hall is in semi-darkness, and still empty. The public arriving by degrees.*

A confusion of voices is heard outside the door. A TROOPER *enters hastily.*

DOORKEEPER. Hi! Where's your money?

TROOPER. I come in free!

DOORKEEPER. Why?

TROOPER. I'm one of His Majesty's Cavalry!

DOORKEEPER [*to* ANOTHER TROOPER]. You?

2ND TROOPER. I don't pay!

DOORKEEPER. But—

2ND TROOPER. I'm a Musketeer.

1ST TROOPER. The play doesn't start until two. Nobody's here. How about some exercise?
    [*They fence with the foils they are carrying.*]

A LACKEY [*entering*]. I say! Flanquin.

ANOTHER [*already arrived*]. Diablot?

1ST LACKEY [*producing a pack of cards*]. Cards. Dice.

2ND LACKEY. All right then, I'm your man!
    [*The* 1ST LACKEY *takes a stub of candle from his pocket, lights it and stands it on the floor.*]

1ST LACKEY. I pinched this from my master.

1ST TROOPER [*receiving a thrust*]. Yes, a hit!

[1]

GUARDSMAN [*to a* SHOP-GIRL].
Nice of you to come before the lights are lit.
[*He puts his arm round her.*]

CARD-PLAYER. Clubs!

GUARDSMAN [*pursuing the girl*].
How about a kiss?

GIRL [*pushing him away*]. They'll see us, surely?

GUARDSMAN [*drawing her to a dark corner*].
Not at all!

A MAN [*unwrapping food*]. It's good to get here early.
You can eat in comfort.

CITIZEN [*shepherding a* BOY]. Come and sit here, my son.

CARD-PLAYER. A triple ace!

CITIZEN [*to his son*]. Wouldn't you think we were in
A den of iniquity! — Drinking!
[*A* FENCER, *stepping back, jostles him.*]
Brawling!
[*He finds himself among the card-players.*]
Gambling!

GUARDSMAN [*still tormenting the girl*].
Give us a kiss!

CITIZEN [*dragging his son away*].
Good heavens! Appalling!
[*A group of* PAGES *come in, singing and dancing.*]

PAGES. Tra la la, tra la la, tra la la, tra la la, lay . . .

DOORKEEPER [*severely, to the* PAGES].
No playing the fool now!

1ST PAGE [*with wounded dignity*]. What a thing to say!
[*Briskly to the* 2ND PAGE *as soon as the* DOORKEEPER's *back is turned.*]
Have you got any string?

2ND PAGE. Yes, and a couple of hooks.

[2]

1st PAGE. If we get up high we can fish for people's perukes.

A PICKPOCKET [*gathering about him some evil-looking youths*].
Now, you young priggers, pay attention, please:
The first principles of robbery are these—

THE BOY [*to his* FATHER].
What's the play this evening, dad?

CITIZEN.   'Clorise.'*

THE BOY. Who wrote it?

CITIZEN.   Balthasar Baro. Oh, a grand piece!

PICKPOCKET.
—and remember to snip off the lace below the knees!

A SPECTATOR [*to another, pointing*].
On the first night of *Le Cid* I sat up there!*

PICKPOCKET [*using his fingers as though picking a pocket*].
Watches like this—

CITIZEN [*to his* SON].   You'll see great actors here—

PICKPOCKET [*making a gesture of pulling at something in little jerks*].
And handkerchiefs—

CITIZEN.   Montfleury—*

SPECTATOR [*from the gallery*].   Let's have some light!

CITIZEN. Bellerose, Jodelet—they all appear tonight!*

PAGE [*in the pit*]. Here's the Orange Girl!

ORANGE GIRL [*appearing from behind the bar*].
                                      Raspberry-water, fruits,
Milk, lemonade—
                        [*A brouhaha at the doors.*]

A HIGH-PITCHED VOICE. Out of the way, you brutes!

1st MARQUIS [*seeing the hall half empty*].
What's this? We arrive like tradesmen, or such as those,
Without disturbing people or treading on toes?

[3]

How disappointing!

[*Recognizing some other gentlemen.*]

Cuigy! Brissaille!

[*Great embracing.*]

CUIGY. That's it—
So faithful, we're here before the lights are lit.

MARQUIS. Don't speak of it! I'm thoroughly put out.

ANOTHER. Cheer up: this man will see to it now, no doubt.

THE CROWD [*applauding the stage-hand come to light up*]. Ah!

[LIGNIÈRE, *a distinguished, though dissipated-looking man, his clothes rather rumpled, enters arm in arm with* CHRISTIAN DE NEUVILLETTE. CHRISTIAN, *elegantly dressed, though a little unfashionably, seems preoccupied, his glance frequently wandering to the boxes.*]

CUIGY. Lignière!

BRISSAILLE [*laughing*]. What! eight o'clock and not drunk *yet*?

LIGNIÈRE [*aside to* CHRISTIAN].
May I introduce you? [CHRISTIAN *nods.*]
The Baron de Neuvillette.
Messieurs de Cuigy, de Brissaille.

CHRISTIAN. Delighted.

1ST MARQUIS [*to the* 2ND].
Personable, but his tailoring's outdated.

LIGNIÈRE [*to* CUIGY].
He comes from Touraine.

CHRISTIAN. Yes, a fortnight ago.
I'm joining the company of Guards tomorrow.

ORANGE GIRL. Oranges, milk—

VIOLINS [*tuning up*]. La . . . la . . .

CUIGY [*to* CHRISTIAN]. The place will be full.

1ST MARQUIS. Everyone's here who is anyone at all.

LIGNIÈRE [*drawing* CHRISTIAN *aside*].
I came to help you out, but I don't think

[4]

The lady is coming. I'll go and get a drink.

CHRISTIAN.
No, don't! You've written songs about all the Court
And Society. You're the one man, I thought,
Who could tell me about this woman who dazzles me.

1ST VIOLIN [*tapping with his bow*].
Gentlemen! [*He raises his bow.*]

ORANGE GIRL. Macaroons, lemonade—
[*The violins start to play.*]

CHRISTIAN.   What puzzles me
Is whether or not she is one of those exquisites
Of the clever kind who would scare me out of my wits.
The way that nowadays they talk and write
Worries me. I'm a soldier, simply that,
And I feel awkward.—She is always there
In that empty seat.

LIGNIÈRE.   I'm going.

CHRISTIAN.   Do stay here!

LIGNIÈRE. I can't. D'Assoucy is waiting across the road*
At the Tavern. I'm dying of thirst.

ORANGE GIRL [*passing with her tray*]. Orangeade!

LIGNIÈRE [*with disgust*].   Good God!

ORANGE GIRL. Milk?

LIGNIÈRE.   Ugh!

ORANGE GIRL.   Bordeaux?

LIGNIÈRE.   Here, wait a bit! That's fine.
[*To* CHRISTIAN.]
I'll stay for a little while!—I'll have some wine.
[*He sits down at the bar.*]
[*The* ORANGE GIRL *pours the wine.*]

CRIES [*from the public as a plump little man enters gaily*].
Ragueneau!

[5]

LIGNIÈRE [*to* CHRISTIAN].
　　　　　The famous pastry-cook Ragueneau.

RAGUENEAU [*to* LIGNIÈRE].
　Monsieur, have you seen Monsieur de Cyrano?

LIGNIÈRE [*introducing him to* CHRISTIAN].
　The pastry-cook-in-chief to every poet
　And actor in the business.

RAGUENEAU.　　　　　　Too kind.

LIGNIÈRE.　　　　　　　　　You know it,
　You patron of the arts!

RAGUENEAU.　　　　　I like to serve them.

LIGNIÈRE. On credit.　And his talents well deserve them,
　He's a poet himself.

RAGUENEAU.　　　　They sometimes tell me so.

LIGNIÈRE. Mad about poetry!

RAGUENEAU.　　　　　　Well, yes, it's true;
　In return for an Ode—

LIGNIÈRE.　　　　　You'd give away a pie.

RAGUENEAU. Oh, a slice, perhaps!

LIGNIÈRE.　　　　Don't be modest, you generous soul.
　And for a triolet—

RAGUENEAU.　　　　It's worth a roll.

LIGNIÈRE. A cream roll, at that. Tell me, are you fond
　Of the theatre?

RAGUENEAU.　　　I adore it, and beyond!

LIGNIÈRE. You pay for the tickets, don't you, with cakes and
　　sweets?
　How much did it cost this evening for your seats,
　Between ourselves? Equivalent to francs and sous.

RAGUENEAU. I can tell you exactly. Four flans. Fifty cachous.
　　　　　[*He looks all around him.*]
　Is Cyrano really not here? I'm surprised at that!

[6]

LIGNIÈRE. Why?

RAGUENEAU.   Montfleury is acting.

LIGNIÈRE.   I know, but what
Does that matter to Cyrano?

RAGUENEAU.   Surely you have heard?
He's forbidden Montfleury, whom he hates like rancid curd,
From appearing again for at least a month.*

LIGNIÈRE [who is on his fourth glass].   And so?

RAGUENEAU. Montfleury is acting!

CUIGY [who has left his group]. There's nothing that he can do.

RAGUENEAU. That's just what I've come to see, you under-
    stand.

1ST MARQUIS. Who is this Cyrano fellow?

CUIGY.   A master hand
At sword fighting.

2ND MARQUIS.   Well born?

CUIGY.   Enough. His friend
Le Bret can tell you more than I can. [Calling]. Ho,
Le Bret!*

            [LE BRET comes up to him.]
            Are you looking for Cyrano?

LE BRET. Yes, I'm worried.

CUIGY.   Isn't he the most unusual man?

LE BRET. He's the most remarkable being under the moon!

RAGUENEAU. Poet!

CUIGY.   Fighter!

BRISSAILLE.   Musician!

LE BRET.   Philosopher!

LIGNIÈRE. With the most anomalous face you ever saw!

RAGUENEAU. True, a grim artist, like Philip of Champaigne,
    Would find painting his portrait quite a strain:
    But Jacques Callot would have been set on fire

[7]

With such a subject: ludicrous, bizarre,
Extravagant: would have made a masterpiece
Out of the plumed hat and the mad grace,
His sword thrusting up from under his cloak
As insolently as a fighting cock,
And proudly above his Puncinello's ruff
Bearing a nose—ah, yes, a nose enough!
On seeing it one thinks 'It can't be true!'
And then, 'Of course, it's held in place with glue:
He'll take it off and put it on the window-sill.'
But dear Monsieur de Bergerac never will.

LE BRET. He carries it—prepared to slice in half
A man who mentions it to raise a laugh!

RAGUENEAU [*proudly*].
The Fates have shears: his sword is half of them.

1ST MARQUIS [*shrugging*].
He won't put in an appearance!

RAGUENEAU.   Yes, he'll come:
I'll wager a chicken à la Ragueneau!

THE MARQUIS [*laughing*]. Done!
[*Murmurs of admiration in the theatre.* ROXANE *has appeared in her box. She seats herself in the front, the* DUENNA *behind her.* CHRISTIAN *suddenly sees her.*]

CHRISTIAN.   Look, there she is, Lignière!

LIGNIÈRE.   And so
That's the lady?

CHRISTIAN.   Yes—do tell me, man,
I've got to know!

LIGNIÈRE.   Madeleine Robin,
Known as Roxane. Artistic. Cultivated.

CHRISTIAN. Alas!

LIGNIÈRE.   Unattached. An orphan. And related
To Cyrano, the man we've been discussing.

[8]

[*At this moment a very distinguished gentleman, wearing the Cordon Bleu, enters the box and stands talking to* ROXANE.]

CHRISTIAN [*agitated*]. Who is that with her?

LIGNIÈRE [*becoming drunk, winking at* CHRISTIAN].

                             Ha! this will set you cursing:
The Count de Guiche, infatuated by her,
But married to the niece of Cardinal Richelieu,
And so is dominated by the one desire
To see Roxane married to a certain dire
Viscount de Valvert, who would make, he knows,
A complaisant spouse. She's determined to refuse;
But de Guiche is such a power in the land
He could make his wishes awkward to withstand.
I've written a song, exposing the whole dirty
Business. It's made him devilish shirty!
There's a sting in the tail. Listen.

    [*He gets up unsteadily, his glass raised, ready to sing.*]

CHRISTIAN.   No. Goodnight.

LIGNIÈRE. Where are you going?

CHRISTIAN.   To see this parasite
De Valvert.

LIGNIÈRE.   He could be the death of you!

          [*He indicates* ROXANE *with his eyes.*]

Stay here. She's looking at you.

CHRISTIAN.   Yes, that's true!

    [*He stands looking at her. The group of* PICKPOCKETS, *seeing him preoccupied and looking up at the box, approach.*]

LIGNIÈRE. Well, dear boy, I must be off. I have an
Awful thirst to see to at the tavern.

              [*He departs zigzaggedly.*]

    [LE BRET, *who has been looking about the theatre, returns to* RAGUENEAU, *reassured.*]

LE BRET. No sign of Cyrano.

RAGUENEAU [*incredulous*].   But all the same . . .

LE BRET. I just hope he hasn't seen Montfleury's name
Announced for tonight.

AUDIENCE. Begin! Begin the play!
[*A* MARQUIS *sees* DE GUICHE *come away from* ROXANE's *box,
surrounded by obsequious noblemen, among them the* VISCOUNT
DE VALVERT.]

MARQUIS. De Guiche is holding court in his usual way!

ANOTHER. Fo! These Gascons!

THE FIRST. Their steely craftiness
Is why they always have so much success.
I think we'd better acknowledge him.
[*They go up to* DE GUICHE.]

2ND MARQUIS. Well, Count,
What beautiful ribbons! I'm afraid I can't
Recall the colour. Is it 'Kiss me, little maid'
Or 'Hart's courage'?

DE GUICHE. Well, this actual shade
Is 'Spaniard's Downfall'.

1ST MARQUIS. And it doesn't lie.
Plenty of Spaniards will fall and die
In Flanders, thanks to your bravery.

DE GUICHE. Shall we take
Our seats? Are you coming?
[*He goes towards the stage, followed by* MARQUISES *and*
GENTLEMEN. *Turning, he calls.*]
Come along, Valvert!

CHRISTIAN [*starting at the name*].
The Viscount! I'll fling in his face my—
[*He puts his hand in his pocket, and finds the hand of the* PICK-
POCKET *about to rob him. He turns round.*]
—Here!
I was looking for a glove!

PICKPOCKET. And found a hand.
[*Changing his tone, whispering rapidly.*]

[10]

Let me go. I'll tell you a secret, friend.

CHRISTIAN [*still holding him*]. What is it?

PICKPOCKET.   The man who just left you—

CHRISTIAN.   Lignière?

PICKPOCKET. Yes—he's as good as dead I hear.
  A song he wrote has offended a noble lord,
  And tonight a hundred men will be out for his blood!

CHRISTIAN. A hundred? Who's paying them?

PICKPOCKET [*mysteriously*].   Etiquette, mate.

CHRISTIAN. What do you mean?

PICKPOCKET [*with great dignity*]. Professional etiquette.

CHRISTIAN. Where will they be posted?

PICKPOCKET.   At the Porte de Nesle.
  It's the way he goes home. Warn him!

CHRISTIAN.   Yes, I will,
  But where shall I find him?

PICKPOCKET.   Make the circular tour
  Of all the taverns: try The Golden Ewer,
  The Pickled Herring, The Bursting Belt, The Two
  Topers, The Three Funnels. If I were you
  I'd leave a note at each, and the job's done.

CHRISTIAN. All right! The bastards! A hundred against one!
        [*Looking up longingly at* ROXANE.]
  But to leave—her!
        [*With a furious look at* VALVERT.]
                    And him! Yet Lignière must be told!
  [*He rushes out.* DE GUICHE *and his followers have gone on to
  the stage to take their seats. The pit is full; so are the galleries
  and boxes.*]

AUDIENCE. Let the play begin!

A CITIZEN [*whose wig flies up on the end of the* PAGE's *fishing-line*].
                                My wig!

CRIES OF JOY.   He's bald!
  Well done, pages! Ha! ha! ha!

CITIZEN [shaking his fist].   Young torment!
    [Loud laughter and shouts, gradually decreasing. Complete silence.]

LE BRET [astonished]. Why this sudden silence?
              [A SPECTATOR whispers to him.]

SPECTATOR.   My informant
  Is genuine.

MURMURS [round the hall]. Has he come?—No!—Do you think
  he will?—
  Yes, in the box behind the lattice grill.—
  The Cardinal? The Cardinal!*—

A PAGE.   The devil,
  Now we can't behave badly, with him here!
      [One knock from the stage. Everyone still and attentive.]

VOICE OF MARQUIS [behind the curtain].
  Snuff that candle!

ANOTHER [looking through curtain]. Will someone fetch a chair?
    [A chair is passed from hand to hand, over the heads of the audi-
    ence. The MARQUIS takes it and disappears, after blowing kisses
    to the boxes. Three knocks on the stage. The curtain opens.
    Tableau. The MARQUISES arrogantly on chairs to left and right.
    The scene: a pastoral landscape. Four small candelabra light the
    stage. The violins play softly.]

LE BRET [in a low voice to RAGUENEAU].
  Montfleury enters first?

RAGUENEAU.   Yes.

LE BRET.   No sign yet
  Of Cyrano. He's not coming.

RAGUENEAU.   I've lost my bet.

LE BRET. That's all to the good. It saves a lot of worry.
    [A tune is heard on the bagpipe, and MONTFLEURY enters, a vast
    man, in the costume of an Arcadian shepherd, a hat trimmed with
    roses dropping over one ear, blowing on a ribboned bagpipe.]

[12]

AUDIENCE. Bravo, bravo! Montfleury! Montfleury!

MONTFLEURY [*bows, and starts to act Phédon*].
  'Happy the man who far from city's strife
  Self-banished lives his solitary life,
  And who by silver streams and forests amber—'

A VOICE [*from the audience*].
  Lout, I've banished you for a month, remember?
      [*Sensation. Everyone turns to look. Murmuring.*]

SEVERAL VOICES. Hey! What? What is it?

CUIGY.   It's him!

LE BRET [*terrified*].   Cyrano!

THE VOICE.   The King
  Of Jesters! Clear the stage!

EVERYBODY [*indignant*].   Oh!

MONTFLEURY.   But—

THE VOICE.   Are you being
  Obstinate?

DIFFERENT VOICES [*from the pit and boxes*].
      Quiet! That's enough!—Continue,
  Montfleury! Show us the courage in you!

MONTFLEURY [*uncertainly*].
  'Happy the man who far from city's—'

THE VOICE [*more menacing*].   Strife?
  Is that what you want? You'll have it, on my life!
    [*A cane is flourished above the heads of the audience.*]

MONTFLEURY [*his voice getting feebler*].
  'Happy the man who—'
        [*The cane thrashes the air.*]

THE VOICE.   Get off!

MONTFLEURY [*choking*].
        'Hap—Hap—Happy the man . . .'
  [CYRANO, *leaping up in the audience on to a chair, his arms folded, his hat cocked fiercely, moustache bristling, his nose terrible.*]

[13]

CYRANO. I'm getting angry!
        [*Sensation in the audience.*]

MONTFLEURY [*to the* MARQUISES]. Help me, gentlemen!

A MARQUIS [*nonchalantly*]. Get *on* with it!

CYRANO. You man of bulk! Any more of that hap—hap
    And I'll come up there and wipe you off the map!

MARQUIS. This is too much! Montfleury—

CYRANO.   Off he gets—
    Or I'll lop his ears and chop him into bits!

A VOICE. Shame!

CYRANO.   Away with him!

ANOTHER VOICE.   Surely—

CYRANO.   Is he still there?
        [*With the gesture of rolling up his sleeves.*]
    I'll puncture him and let out all the air!

MONTFLEURY [*trying to be dignified*].
    When you insult me, you insult the Muse
    Of Comedy!

CYRANO.   Should that lady ever choose
    To condescend to glance at you, her eyes
    Would take one look of horror at your size
    And kick you with her buskin-boot, to prove
    That she's a worthy daughter of great Jove.

THE PIT. Montfleury! Montfleury! Go on with the play!

CYRANO. Be careful, now—don't put me in a rage:
    My sword is restive!

CROWD [*drawing back*]. Watch him!

CYRANO [*to* MONTFLEURY].   Leave the stage!

CROWD [*coming nearer, grumbling*].
    Oh! Oh!

A LADY [*in the boxes*].
            Outrageous!

[14]

A LORD.   Scandalous!

A BOURGEOIS.   *I* don't know!

A PAGE. What a lark!

THE PIT.   Kss! Montfleury!—Cyrano!

CYRANO. Silence!

THE PIT [*delirious with excitement*].

                    Quack, quack! Baa! Cockadoodledoo!

CYRANO. Listen!

A PAGE.   Miaow!

CYRANO.   Be quiet, all of you!
  I'll issue a challenge to every man that's here.
  Let's have your names! Is no one going to stir?
  Who'll head the list? Will you, sir? No? You, there,
  Will you? No! The first to volunteer
  I'll dispatch with all the honours at my command.
  —Whoever wants to die put up his hand.
                    [*Silence*.]
  Does a naked weapon shock your modesty?
  No offers? Not a finger?—Now, where were we?
  [*He turns towards the stage where* MONTFLEURY *waits in
  agony*.]
  I want this carbuncle out of the theatre
  Or else . . . [*His hand on his sword.*]
                    . . . the scalpel.

MONTFLEURY.   But I—I—

CYRANO.   And it will be at a
  Clap of the hands. I'll clap three times, and on
  The third clap this supervacaneous moon
  Will be eclipsed.

THE PIT [*amused*].   Ah!

CYRANO [*clapping hands*]. One!

MONTFLEURY.   I—

A VOICE [*from the boxes*].   Stay!

[15]

THE PIT. He stays—he goes—he stays—

MONTFLEURY.   I think I may,
  Gentlemen—

CYRANO.   Two!

MONTFLEURY.   I think it's better—

CYRANO.   Three!
  [MONTFLEURY *disappears as though through a trap-door. A*
  storm of laughter, whistling, etc.]

THE CROWD. Boo! Coward! Come back!

CYRANO [*delighted, sitting back in a chair*].
                    Let him come back, if he dare!

A CITIZEN. Call the Manager!
              [BELLEROSE *comes forward and bows.*]

THE BOXES.   Ah, Bellerose is here!

BELLEROSE [*elegantly*]. My noble lords—

THE PIT.   No, we want Jodelet!

JODELET [*coming forward, nasally*].
  Groundlings—

THE PIT.   Bravo! Bravo! Well, what do you say?

JODELET. It's not bravo at all. That solid man
  Whose bulk you loved, was taken—

THE PIT.   The coward ran!

JODELET. —felt he should withdraw . . .

THE PIT.   Fetch him back again!

SOME. No!

OTHERS. Yes!

A YOUNG MAN [*to* CYRANO]. Monsieur, could you explain
  Why you've taken such a scunner against this man?

CYRANO. There are two reasons, and both are excellent.
  First, he's a terrible actor who likes to rant:
  He heaves up his lines like a dredger scooping mud,

[16]

When the verse should be allowed to lift and scud.
Second—well, that's my business.

AN OLD CITIZEN [*behind him*].   That's all very well,
  But we came to see the play!

CYRANO.   The play is hell.

BELLEROSE. What about the entrance money to be returned?

CYRANO. Bellerose, that's the most intelligent thing I've heard!
  Never let it be said the Arts lacked my support.
          [*He rises and throws a bag of money.*]
  Here, catch, and now shut up!

AUDIENCE [*dazzled*].   Ah! Oh! Well caught!
          [JODELET *catches the purse and weighs it in his hand.*]

JODELET. Sir, on these terms, you have my permission to close
  The performance down on any night you choose!

BELLEROSE. Ladies and gentlemen, you will kindly leave
  The theatre.

JODELET.   In an orderly manner, please!
          [*The people begin to go out, while* CYRANO *looks on with satis-
          faction. But the crowd stop on hearing the following scene and
          remain where they are.*]

LE BRET [*to* CYRANO]. You're insane!

THE BUSYBODY [*approaching* CYRANO].

                                The actor Montfleury! I say
  It's scandalous! Why, he's the protégé
  Of the Duke of Candale. And who's *your* patron?

CYRANO. Nobody.

BUSYBODY.   You mean you haven't one?

CYRANO. No!

BUSYBODY.   No man of influence as protector?

CYRANO. I've said No to that twice. Do you expect a
  Third? No, I have no patronizing lord:
  Only this guardian angel here, my sword.

BUSYBODY. You'll get out of town, then?

CYRANO.   That all depends.

BUSYBODY. The Duke has a long arm.

CYRANO [showing his sword].   But mine extends
  Even further, you see.

BUSYBODY.   You'd never contemplate—

CYRANO. I might.

BUSYBODY.   But—

CYRANO.   Now suppose you ambulate.

BUSYBODY. But—

CYRANO.   Off you go!—Or, rather, tell me why
  You're staring at my nose.

BUSYBODY [abashed].   Excuse me, I—

CYRANO. Does it surprise you?

BUSYBODY.   Your honour mustn't think—

CYRANO. Does it swing like an elephant's prehensile trunk?

BUSYBODY. I haven't said—

CYRANO.   Is it curved like an owl's beak?
  Do you see a pimple on it?

BUSYBODY.   I didn't speak—

CYRANO. Is a fly sauntering there? What's the curiosity?

BUSYBODY. Oh! . . .

CYRANO.   Do you consider it an atrocity?

BUSYBODY. I've been so careful not to look at it!

CYRANO.   Why
  Have you been so careful not to look at it, pray?

BUSYBODY. I was told—

CYRANO.   Does it repel you, then?

BUSYBODY.   Monsieur—

CYRANO. Do you find it an unhealthy colour?

BUSYBODY. Monsieur!

CYRANO.   Is the shape obscene?

[18]

BUSYBODY.   Certainly not!

CYRANO. Then what's this criticism all about?
   —Perhaps you find it a little bit too big?

BUSYBODY [*stammering*].
   I find it small, quite small, *tiny*!

CYRANO.   A plague
   On that! An absurd small nose, you now inform us!
   Small? My nose?

BUSYBODY.   O heavens!

CYRANO.   It's enormous!
   —It's time you learnt, you pug-nosed, flat-headed,
   Plate-faced scoundrel, that I'm proudly wedded
   To this nose I've got. A big nose is the sign
   Of a good, courteous, intelligent, benign,
   Liberal, courageous man: such as you see
   Before you, and such as you will never be
   Even in your own opinion, you puerile wreck!
   Because that inglorious face on the top of your neck
   Which I now salute— [*He slaps him.*]

BUSYBODY.   Ow!

CYRANO.   —is as utterly devoid
   Of aspiration, lyricism, pride,
   Sparkle, magnificence—of Nose, in short—
   [*He turns him round by the shoulders, suiting the action to the
   word.*]
   As those other cheeks which now will feel my boot!

BUSYBODY [*running away*].
   Help! Guards!

CYRANO.   A warning to the unwise
   Who criticize the centre of my face.
   And if he's a nobleman, manners require
   That I attack him from the front, and higher,
   And give him, before he leaves me altogether,
   The argument of steel instead of leather!

[19]

DE GUICHE [*who has come down with the* MARQUIS].
   He's becoming a nuisance!

VISCOUNT DE VALVERT [*shrugging*]. He's a swaggering fool!

DE GUICHE. Will nobody deflate him?

VISCOUNT.   Yes! I will.
   I'll whip him with my tongue until he is sorry!
        [*He advances on* CYRANO *who is watching him.*]
   Your . . . hm . . . your nose . . . your nose is large.

CYRANO [*gravely*].   Yes, very.

VISCOUNT [*laughing*]. Ha!

CYRANO.   Is that all?

VISCOUNT.   What?

CYRANO.   That the best you can do?
   Ah, no! There's a vast choice. I'll supply a few
   Alternatives. For instance, if you chose
   The Approach Aggressive: 'Sir, if I had your nose
   I'd amputate it!' Or the Kindly, say:
   'When drinking don't you find it gets in the way?
   You need a kind of trough of a special shape.'
   Descriptive: 'It's a rock—a peak—a cape.
   Did I say "cape"? An entire peninsula!'
   Curious: 'What precisely do you use it for?
   A pencil-box? Or perhaps a razor-cover?'
   Gracious: 'You must be a passionate bird-lover
   That you're so anxious to provide a site
   Where feathered friends can safely roost at night.'
   The Approach Truculent: 'Surely when you smoke
   Your pipe, the fumes will make the neighbours choke
   And rush round screaming "A chimney is on fire!" '
   The Approach Considerate: 'Take care when you admire
   The ladies. If you bow your nose too far
   Gravity's force will drag you to the floor.'
   The Tender: 'You should have a sunshade made.

I fear the sunlight makes the colours fade.'
Pedantic: 'Only the beast that Aristophanes
Called Hippocamelelephantoles
Could rival so much flesh on so much bone.'
Or should you prefer a more Contemptuous tone:
'Is it the fashion to go about with that on?
So very convenient to hang your hat on.'
Emphatic: 'You needn't fear the chilling breeze.
Only a howling gale could make you sneeze.'
Dramatic: 'If it bled, we'd drown in the Red Sea.'
Admiring: 'What a perfumer's shop-sign it would be!'
Lyric: 'Is this the conch-shell the Tritons blew?'
Naive: 'What time is the Monument on view?'
The Approach Respectful: 'My mind's quite out of joint.
In which direction does your signpost point?'
Rustic: 'Is that a nose, maister? I dursel
Swear it's a pumpkin or a mangol-wurzel.'
Military: 'Your halberd at the ready!'
Practical: 'Grab hold when you're unsteady.'
Or Pyramus with Thisbe by the wall:
'I kiss your nose-hole, not your lips at all!'
—Such, my dear sir, is what you might have said
If there was a grain of wit inside your head.
As man of letters you're hardly a success;
The only three you have are A-S-S.
But O, O most lamentable of mokes,
If by some miracle you had cracked those jokes
To entertain us—well, all jokes are killable:
You wouldn't have got beyond the second syllable.
I can serve myself with quips like these for ever,
But let another person try it?—Never!

DE GUICHE [*trying to draw the* VISCOUNT *away*]. Let him be.

VISCOUNT [*raging*]. Such arrogance!—in a lout
    Who . . . doesn't even wear gloves, and goes about
    Without bows or ribbons!

[21]

CYRANO.   My finery's in the heart.
  I don't have to dress myself like a male tart.
  Or flaunt my cuffs to demonstrate my merit.
  My plumage is an independent spirit,
  A plume to brave all weathers, my panache!*
  I twirl my points of wit like a moustache,
  And cross the city's sycophantic squares
  Making Truth ring as others clank their spurs.
  It isn't the well-cut suit but the well-cut mind
  And deeds, not frills, that suit me best, I find.

VISCOUNT. But, sir—

CYRANO.   I wear no gloves? My hands are bare!
  I did have *one*, one of an ancient pair,
  But carelessly I threw the thing away
  In an insolent face which had too much to say.

VISCOUNT. Rascal, jackanapes, flat-footed fool!

CYRANO [*sweeping off his hat*].
  Yes? And I am Cyrano-Savinien-Hercule
  De Bergerac.

VISCOUNT [*infuriated*]. Sir, you're a buffoon!

CYRANO [*as though in agony*].
  Ah!—oo!—ooo!—forgive the moan!

VISCOUNT [*turning round on him*].
  What was that you said to me, you pup?

CYRANO. I've got to shift it! It's started stiffening up!
  This comes of letting it lie here in the damp.
  Ow!

VISCOUNT. What's wrong?

CYRANO.   My sword has got the cramp!

VISCOUNT [*drawing his sword*]. So be it!

CYRANO.   I'll show you a weapon with a soul!

VISCOUNT [*contemptuously*]. Poet!

CYRANO.   Yes, sir, poet!—and in that rôle
   I'll improvise a ballad while we're fighting.

VISCOUNT. A ballad?

CYRANO.   You may not know that style of writing.
   Three verses of eight lines. And then a coda
   Of four lines more—to add the dash of soda.

VISCOUNT. You—

CYRANO.   I'll assemble the poem as we go
   And hit home on the final couplet.

VISCOUNT.   No!

CYRANO. No? [Declaiming.] 'The Ballad of the Duel Fought
   Between de Bergerac and the Figure Nought.'

VISCOUNT. What's that?

CYRANO.   The title!

CROWD [in wild excitement].   Clear a space! Here's fun!
   Choose where you want to be! Get settled down!
       [A circle of interested spectators in the pit. The PAGES climb on
       each other's shoulders to get a better view. The WOMEN standing
       up in the boxes. To the right, DE GUICHE and his retinue. Left,
       DE BRET, RAGUENEAU, CYRANO, etc.]

CYRANO [closing his eyes a moment].
   Wait! Let me pick my rhymes . . . There, let's begin.
       [He fights in time with the words.]
           I swiftly toss away my hat,
           And then, more slowly, I untie
           My trailing cloak to follow that.
           Then from the scabbard on my thigh
           I draw my sword and raise it high—
           And now the blade begins to flit
           And flash like swallows in the sky,
           And at the Coda's end I hit!

           Better for you if you'd kept mum!
           Where shall I catch you, butterfly?

[23]

Across your pericranium,
Below the heart or on the thigh?
There in the groin? Or shall we try
To pierce your finery to the tit?
I'll keep the guts for bye-and-bye
When at the Coda's end I hit!

I need a rhyme for one more verse!
You've gone as pale as winter sky.
Courage beginning to disperse?
Your stroke went wide, I wonder why?
Your vision blurs? Your mouth is dry?
It's wiser to preserve your spit!
I press you, fast as minutes fly,
And at the Coda's end I hit!

[*He announces solemnly.*] CODA:

Prince, pray God to pardon you!
I lunge, I skirmish for a bit,
I parry, I feint—one, two, one, two!
And at the Coda's end—I hit!

[*Acclamation and applause. Flowers and handkerchiefs are thrown down. The* OFFICERS *surround* CYRANO, *congratulating him.* RAGUENEAU *dances for joy.* LE BRET *is happy but anxious. The* VISCOUNT'*s friends support him and move him away.*]

CROWD [*with one long shout*]. Ah!

TROOPER.   Superb!

RAGUENEAU.   Staggerblasting!

A WOMAN.   Bravo!

LE BRET. Madness!

OTHERS.   Congratulations!

A WOMAN'S VOICE.   My hero!

MUSKETEER [*coming to* CYRANO, *hand extended*].
Monsieur, please let me shake you by the hand.

Fighting is something that I understand.
I stamped with pleasure while it was going on.

CYRANO. What's his name, that fellow?

CUIGY. D'Artagnan.*

LE BRET [*to* CYRANO, *taking his arm*].
Let's talk this over.

CYRANO. Wait till they've gone away.
[*To* BELLEROSE.]
Do you mind our waiting?

BELLEROSE [*respectfully*]. Of course not.

JODELET [*looking off*]. Here, I say!
They're hooting Montfleury!

BELLEROSE [*solemnly*]. So glory passes!
[*To the* PORTERS.] Just tidy up a bit and wash the glasses.
You can leave the lights. We're going to rehearse
After supper for tomorrow evening's farce.
[JODELET *and* BELLEROSE *go, after bowing to* CYRANO.]

PORTER [*to* CYRANO].
Are you staying to supper?

CYRANO. No.
[*The* PORTER *goes.*]

LE BRET. Why not?

CYRANO. Because—
[*Seeing the* PORTER *has gone.*]
Because I'm not so wealthy as I was.
I haven't a sou!

LE BRET [*miming the purse-throwing*].
What price that chinking purse?

CYRANO. Vanished in a day!

LE BRET. Then how do you propose
To live until next month?

CYRANO. On air and moisture.

LE BRET. Throwing money away, what folly!

[25]

CYRANO.   But what a gesture!

THE ORANGE-GIRL. Ahem! Monsieur, it makes my heart fair
      bleed
   To think of you not eating. Folk must feed,
   So help yourself.

CYRANO [*removing his hat*]. Dear child, my Gascon pride
   Tells me your offer ought to be denied.
   But rather than upset you, as I might,
   I will accept, perhaps, a modest bite.
                  [*He goes to the buffet.*]
   This grape . . .
                  [*She offers him the whole bunch.*]
                  Just one! . . . This glass of water—
                  [*She offers to pour wine.*]
                                                —neat!
   And half a macaroon. [*He breaks off half for her.*]
                  A meal complete!

LE BRET. Ridiculous!

ORANGE-GIRL.   Do take some more.

CYRANO.   Well, yes.
   I think I will. I'll take your hand to kiss.
      [*He kisses her hand as though she were a princess.*]

ORANGE-GIRL. Thank you, monsieur. [*Curtseying.*] Good-night.
                  [*She goes.*]

CYRANO [*to* LE BRET].   Now fire ahead!
      [*He stands at the buffet and arranges things in front of him.*]

CYRANO. Food! [*Placing the macaroon.*]
                  Water! [*The glass of water.*]
                        Dessert! [*The grape.*] The table's laid!
   My word, I was simply ravenous! [*Eating.*] Go on.

LE BRET. If you pay attention to these dangerous fops
   You'll sow a world of teeth instead of crops.
   Ask anyone with commonsense, he'll say
   What the effect will be of this display.

CYRANO [*finishing the macaroon*]. Colossal.

LE BRET.   The Cardinal—

CYRANO [*radiant*].   Oh, was he there?

LE BRET. He must have thought you—

CYRANO.   —original and rare.

LE BRET. Still—

CYRANO.   He's an author. He should be overjoyed
   To see another writer's play destroyed.

LE BRET. You've acquired a pack of enemies, I'm afraid.

CYRANO. How many, roughly, would you think I've made?

LE BRET. Forty-eight,
   Without counting the women.

CYRANO.   Enumerate.

LE BRET. De Guiche, the Viscount, Baro, Montfleury,
   All the members of the Academy—

CYRANO. Say no more! I'm rapturous!

LE BRET.   But where
   Is all this going to lead, and why do you do it?

CYRANO. Life was a maze; and which way to get through it
   Offered so many alternatives, I might
   Have stood for ever looking left and right.
   And so I took—

LE BRET.   Well, what did you take?

CYRANO.   A shot
   At simply being superb at the whole lot!

LE BRET. I see. Now tell the truth, why do you hate
   Montfleury so?

CYRANO.   That roll of lard?—so fat
   He can't reach round himself to touch his navel.
   He still imagines himself the very devil
   Where women are concerned, and, all the while

[27]

He's hamming away up there, he makes his vile
Fish-eyes at them. I've loathed him ever since
I caught him ogling *her*. Does it make you wince
To see a slug crawling across a flower?

LE BRET. What? Is it possible?

CYRANO.   That I can love?
It is.

LE BRET. And may one know? You've never said . . .

CYRANO. Who? Just imagine. Any dreams I had
Of being loved have always ended poorly
Because this nose arrived ten minutes early.
So, in the mocking way of things, I'm fated
To love the loveliest woman God created.

LE BRET. Heavens! Who is she?

CYRANO.   She's a mortal danger,
Not knowing that she is; an innocent stranger
To any awareness of her qualities;
A blameless snare of nature, where love lies
Concealed at ambush in a candid rose.
And any man who sees her smiling knows
The meaning of perfection. So much grace
In things inconsequential, that the face
Of heaven glows in the slightest thing she does.

LE BRET. Now everything is clear!

CYRANO.   Diaphanous!

LE BRET. Your cousin, Madeleine Robin?

CYRANO.   Roxane!

LE BRET. Splendid. You love her—the next step is plain:
Tell her so. It was very clear tonight
You clothed yourself with glory in her sight.

CYRANO. Look at me, friend. What hope can I ever have
With this protuberance pointing to my grave?
I can't deceive myself. Oh, yes, I stroll
Sometimes in an evening garden, and inhale

[28]

With this great devil nose the promises
Of April. And I watch young couples pass
Arm in arm; and dream of walking soon
With one beside me under a brilliant moon.
I feel transfigured! And then my damned eyes fall
On my profile's shadow against the garden wall.

LE BRET [*moved*]. My friend!

CYRANO.　　　　　　My friend, such painful hours I've known,
Feeling myself unsightly, and alone.

LE BRET [*taking his hand*]. Are you crying?

CYRANO.　　　　　　　　　　Never! I revere
Sorrow far too much to let a tear
Slide down this comic slope. No; tears are fine
On beauty's cheek, but out of place on mine!

LE BRET. Don't be unhappy. You must have noticed how
Pleased the little barmaid was just now
When you kissed her hand.

CYRANO.　　　　　　That's true.

LE BRET.　　　　　　　　　　Well, then!—Roxane
Went white as a sheet while she was looking on.

CYRANO. Did she?

LE BRET.　　　　She's heart and soul already half
Prepared. Be brave. Ask her.

CYRANO.　　　　　　　And see her laugh?
That's the only thing in the world I really fear.

PORTER [*entering with the* DUENNA].
A lady to see you, sir.

CYRANO.　　　　　Her Duenna's here!

DUENNA [*with a deep curtsey*].
Someone wants to know where one could meet
One's valiant cousin, keeping it discreet.

CYRANO [*boulversé*]. Meet?

DUENNA [*curtseying again*].
                    There are certain things one would like to say.

CYRANO. Things?

DUENNA [*again a curtsey*]. Private matters.

CYRANO [*tottering*].   My God!

DUENNA.   At break of day
  One will go to Mass ...

CYRANO.   My God!

DUENNA.   So afterwards
  Where would be a good place for a few words?

CYRANO [*confused*].
  Where? I—but—oh, my God!

DUENNA.   Where would you say?

CYRANO. I'm thinking! ... At—Ragueneau's—the confec-
  tioner.

DUENNA. Where's that?

CYRANO.   In the Rue—My God!—Saint-Honoré.

DUENNA. Well, be there at seven, then.

CYRANO.   Yes, I'll be there.
    [*Exit the* DUENNA. CYRANO *falls into* LE BRET'*s arms.*]

CYRANO. I! She! A rendezvous!

LE BRET.   Call it a tryst.
  Are you happy now?

CYRANO.   She knows that I exist!

LE BRET. Now I hope you'll be calm.

CYRANO.   Be calm? What, *now*?
  I shall be volcanic!—bellicose!
  I want an entire army to oppose!
  I have ten hearts, and twenty arms; I'm past
  Coping with humans—[*wildly*]—I need something vast!
    [*For a few moments the* ACTORS *have been moving about the
    stage whispering. Rehearsal is beginning. The* FIDDLERS *are in
    their places.*]

VOICE [*from the stage*].
  Quiet, everyone, please! Rehearsal has begun.

CYRANO [*laughing*].
  All right, we're off!
    [*He moves away.* CUIGY, BRISSAILLE *and some* OFFICERS
    enter by the big door, supporting LIGNIÈRE *who is very drunk.*]

CUIGY.   Cyrano!

CYRANO.   What's going on?

CUIGY. We've brought you an enormous sponge.

CYRANO.   Lignière!
  What's wrong with him? And what's he doing here?

CUIGY. In such a state! He's been out looking for you.

BRISSAILLE. Afraid to go home.

CYRANO.   But why?

LIGNIÈRE [*showing a crumpled letter*]. Look—I implore you—
  Had this letter . . . warning me . . . a hundred strong . . .
  Waiting to get me . . . just because of that song . . .
  In terrible danger . . . Porte de Nesle . . . the way I
  Have to go home . . . Will sleep at *your* house . . . May I?

CYRANO. A hundred men? You'll sleep in your own bed!

LIGNIÈRE [*frightened*]. But—

CYRANO [*in a terrible voice*]. Take that lantern!
    [LIGNIÈRE *grabs the lantern.*]
                              Now we march ahead!
  I'll see you tucked-up safely, never fear.
                [*To the* OFFICERS.]
  Follow, as witnesses—don't come too near.

CUIGY. But a hundred men!

CYRANO.   A pity there aren't more!
    [*The* ACTORS *and* ACTRESSES, *in their costumes, have come
    down from the stage and are listening.*]

LE BRET. But why protect—

CYRANO.   Grumbling again? What for?

LE BRET. —this worthless drunk?

CYRANO [slapping LIGNIÈRE on the shoulder].
                          Because this worthless drunk,
This cask of wine, this saturated trunk,
Once did a deed of grace that I find a pearl:
Leaving the church one day, he saw his girl
Using the holy water. Then this man,
Who loathes water of any vintage, ran
Back to the stoup and drained it dry!

COMEDIENNE.   How charming!

CYRANO. Yes, I have always thought it quite disarming.

COMEDIENNE [to the others].
One poor little poet against a hundred men!

CYRANO [to the OFFICERS].
As for you, gentlemen, don't muscle in
When you see them attacking. This is my affair.

ANOTHER COMEDIENNE. I must come and watch!

CYRANO.   Come, then!

ANOTHER [to an old ACTOR].   Will you, Pierre?

CYRANO. You'd better all come—make it a carnival,
Folly and wisdom, life fantastical
With tragedy implicit, and the beat
Of hearts and bells and drums and dancing feet!

ALL THE WOMEN [dancing for joy].
Bravo! Let's get our cloaks!

JODELET.   The fun begins!

CYRANO. Play us a tune, friends, on your violins!
    [The FIDDLERS join the procession. They use the footlights for
    torches.]

CYRANO [ordering the ranks].
Well done! The Officers here, then the ladies come,
And ahead of you all—I, alone, with my plume

[32]

Like glory itself careening above my hat,
As proud as Scipio or a Persian cat!
—Do you understand? Nobody interferes!
Ready? One, two, three! Open the doors!
  [*The* PORTER *opens the great doors; a view of Paris in moon-
  light.*]
Ah! Paris at night, a dream half lost in sleep:
The roofs are like bright shields braving the moon,
True backcloth for this call-to-arms we keep,
While the Seine flows mysteriously down
With boats and stars and lamplight to the sea.
The advance begins, and what will be will be!

ALL. To the Porte de Nesle!

CYRANO [*standing on the threshold*]. To the Porte de Nesle!
          [*He turns to the* COMEDIENNE.]
You were asking for the reason, mademoiselle,
Why a hundred men should threaten one poor poet?
          [*He draws his sword; then, calmly:*]
It's because he's a friend of mine, and the bullies know it!
  [*He goes.* LIGNIÈRE *reels after him, followed by the* ACTRESSES
  on the arms of the OFFICERS, *and the* ACTORS; *the violins
  playing.*]

CURTAIN

ACT TWO

RAGUENEAU's *bakery and confectionery shop. The street outside can be seen in the early morning light through the glass door.*

On the left, in the foreground, a counter with an iron stand hung with geese, ducks and white peacocks. Tall bouquets of sunflowers in large china pots. On the same side, further back, a vast open fireplace; in front of it, between huge fire-dogs, roasts dripping into pans. On the right another door. Further back, a staircase leading to a little room under the roof. In this room, seen through an open shutter, a table is laid, candle-lit. It is a place for eating and drinking. A wooden gallery at the top of the staircase leads to other little rooms.

In the middle of the shop an iron hoop hangs from the ceiling. It can be drawn up and down; game hangs from it. The ovens in the shadow of the stairs glow red. The copper pans shine. The spits are turning. Heaps of food piled pyramidally. Hams hanging. It is the busy hour of the morning. Bustle and scurry of scullions, fat cooks and diminutive apprentices, their caps decorated with cocks-feathers and wings of guinea-fowl. They are bringing in heaped up plates of cakes and tarts. Tables laden with rolls and dishes of food. Chairs round other tables wait for the customers.

RAGUENEAU *is sitting at a table, writing.*

1ST COOK [*carrying in a dish*]. Trifle!

2ND COOK. Flan!

3RD COOK. Peacock!

4TH COOK. Rissoles!

5TH COOK. Brawn!

RAGUENEAU [*putting down his pen*].
The copper pans gleam in the light of dawn!

Stifle the Muse, Ragueneau: business governs.
Unstring the lyre, and superintend the ovens!

[*He rises. To a* COOK.]

That sauce looks metrically incomplete!

THE COOK. How?

RAGUENEAU.   To scan it needs another beat. [*He passes on.*]

THE COOK. Huh?

RAGUENEAU [*in front of the range*].

O Muse, avert thine eyes of wild desire
From gazing on this Acheronian fire!

[*To a* COOK *showing him loaves.*]

This loaf's lopsided where you've placed the nicks—
Caesuras should bisect the hemistychs!

[*To* ANOTHER *who shows him an unfinished confection.*]

This palace needs a roof: attend to it.

[*To a* YOUNG APPRENTICE, *who is sitting on the ground
putting poultry on a long spit.*]

Now you, boy, threading on your lengthy spit
This modest pullet and this splendid turkey—
Remember what Malherbe did when at work, he
Alternates the long lines with the short—
So roast your poultry in the way he taught!

ANOTHER APPRENTICE [*coming up with a tray covered by a napkin*].

Master, I hope it's something you'll admire;
I made it to please you.

[*He uncovers the tray, showing a confection in the shape of a
lyre.*]

RAGUENEAU.   A poet's lyre!

APPRENTICE. In almond paste.

RAGUENEAU [*enchanted*].   With candied fruits!

APPRENTICE.   I made
The strings of sugar to look as though they played.

RAGUENEAU [*giving him money*].

You have a natural genius for the trade.

Go and drink my health!
                    [*Seeing* LISE *who has entered.*]
                              Ssh! Here's my wife. No word
About the money!
                [*To* LISE, *casually showing her the lyre.*]
                          Nice, don't you think?
LISE.   Absurd!
          [LISE *places a pile of paper bags on the counter.*]
RAGUENEAU. Paper bags? Thanks.
  [*He looks at them.*]   Good God, this can't be borne!
The poems of my friends, my precious manuscripts, torn
To make biscuit-bags! You're just like one of those grim
Bacchantes who tore Orpheus limb from limb!

LISE [*drily*]. Those limping lines were all we ever got
In payment out of that good-for-nothing lot,
So why shouldn't I use 'em? What's to stop us?

RAGUENEAU. Ant! Don't insult these Olympian grasshoppers!

LISE. Until they started coming here you'd never
Have called me Ant and Bacchante, Master Clever.

RAGUENEAU. To treat poetry like this!

LISE.   How else, God knows!

RAGUENEAU. I dread to think what you do with prose.
                [TWO CHILDREN *have come into the shop.*]

RAGUENEAU. Can I help you, my dears?

IST CHILD.   We want three pies.

RAGUENEAU [*serving them*].
  There, piping hot.

2ND CHILD.   Would you wrap them for us, please?

RAGUENEAU [*aside*].
  It breaks my heart!
  [*To the* CHILDREN.] You really want them wrapped?
    [*He takes a bag, and as he is about to put in the pies he stops to
    read.*]

[36]

'Ulysses, when from the Circean isle escaped . . .'
Not that one!
[*He puts it aside and takes another. Again as he is about to put
in the pies he reads.*]
                    'Auroral Phoebus . . .' No, nor that!

LISE [*impatiently*].
Don't keep the children waiting!

RAGUENEAU.   All right, all right!
[*He takes a third and resigns himself.*]
Sonnet to Phyllis!—It's very hard, I feel!

LISE. Thank goodness you've decided. [*Shrugging.*] Imbecile!
[*She climbs on a chair and starts to arrange plates.*]

RAGUENEAU [*to the departing* CHILDREN].
Here—children! Bring the Sonnet back to me,
And you can have six pies instead of three.
[*The* CHILDREN *quickly make the exchange, and* RAGUENEAU,
smoothing out the paper, starts to read again.]
'Phyllis!'—a spot of grease on that lovely name!
'Phyllis!'—
                    [CYRANO *comes hurrying in.*]

CYRANO.   What time is it?

RAGUENEAU.   Six.

CYRANO [*with emotion*].   In one hour's time!
                    [*He paces up and down the shop.*]

RAGUENEAU [*following him*].
Congratulations!

CYRANO.   On what?

RAGUENEAU.   Your fight.

CYRANO.   Which? Where?

RAGUENEAU. At the Hôtel de Bourgogne!

CYRANO [*disdainfully*].   Oh, that affair!

RAGUENEAU [*admiring*].
The duel in verse!

[37]

LISE.   He says he'll never forget—

CYRANO. What nonsense!

RAGUENEAU [*making passes with a spit*].
                           'At the Coda's end I hit!'
'At the Coda's end I hit!'—it's great, you know!
                     [*With increasing enthusiasm.*]
'At the Coda's end . . .'

CYRANO.   What's the time, Ragueneau?

RAGUENEAU [*stopping his swordplay to look at the clock*].
     Five past six . . . 'I hit!'—It must be grand
To write a ballad!

LISE [*to* CYRANO].   What have you done to your hand?

CYRANO. Nothing. A cut.

RAGUENEAU.   Have you run into trouble?

CYRANO.   No,
     No trouble.

LISE.   I think he's lying.

CYRANO.   Do you, though?
     Did my nose twitch? If so it must have been
A whopping lie!
[*Changing his tone.*] I'm waiting here for someone.
And whatever happens, Judgement Day apart,
See that we're alone.

RAGUENEAU.   I can't, dear heart:
     My poets are coming.

LISE [*ironically*].   To whet their appetite!

CYRANO. Well, when I signal, whisk them out of sight—
     The time?

RAGUENEAU. Ten past.
     [CYRANO *sits down nervously at* RAGUENEAU's *table and takes some paper.*]

CYRANO.   A pen?

[38]

RAGUENEAU [*taking the quill from behind his ear*].
                              Plucked from a swan.
          [A MUSKETEER, *superbly moustached, enters.*]
MUSKETEER [*stentorianly*].
   'Morning! [LISE *hurries to him.*]
CYRANO [*turning round*]. Who's that?
RAGUENEAU.   He's Lise's friend, a man
   Who's a stupendous fighter, or so he says.
CYRANO [*taking up the pen*].
   Ssh! . . . [*To himself.*] I have to write it--that's all it is—
   And give it to her, and go . . . [*Throwing down the pen.*]
                              Coward! But how
   Should I dare to speak one word?— [*To* RAGUENEAU.]
                              What's the time now?
RAGUENEAU. A quarter past.
CYRANO [*beating his breast*]. —one word of all that I might:
   Whereas writing about it . . . [*He takes up the pen again.*]
                              Very well, I'll write.
   It's a love-letter I've written in my mind
   A hundred times: the words all ready to find.
   If I put my heart beside the paper, then
   I have nothing to do but simply to copy it down.
      [*He writes. Behind the glass door can be seen the silhouettes of
      thin figures hesitating outside.*
      The POETS, *dressed in rusty black, their stockings half down,
      covered in mud.*]
LISE [*entering, to* RAGUENEAU].
   Here come your filthy friends!
1ST POET [*entering, to* RAGUENEAU].
                              Brother in art!
2ND POET. Dear colleague!
3RD POET.   Golden eagle of the fiery
   Ovens! [*He sniffs.*] Delicious smells nest in your eyrie!
4TH POET. O Phoebus of the roasting rays!

                         [39]

5TH POET. Apollo
Of confectionery!

RAGUENEAU [*surrounded, embraced, buffeted.*]
How instantly a fellow
Can be at his ease with them!

1ST POET. We were held up
Because of the crowd swarming all over the shop
At the Porte de Nesle.

2ND POET. Eight ruffians lying there
Bleeding, gashed by a sword.

CYRANO [*raising his head for a second*].
Eight? I could swear
There were only seven. [*He returns to his letter.*]

RAGUENEAU [*to* CYRANO]. Any idea who
This hero was?

CYRANO [*casually*]. I? No!

LISE [*to the* MUSKETEER]. Have you?

MUSKETEER [*twirling his moustache*].
Perhaps!

CYRANO [*writing, to himself*].
'I love you . . .'

1ST POET. As I understand it
One man scattered the whole gang single-handed!

2ND POET. A quite extraordinary sight! We found
Pikes and cudgels littering the ground!

CYRANO. 'Your eyes . . .'

3RD POET. We were picking up hats and strips
Of clothing as far as the Quai des Orfèvres!

CYRANO. '. . . your lips . . .'

1ST POET. He must be a titan, this man, whoever he was!

CYRANO. 'And . . . And I'm ready to faint with fear when I
see you because . . .'

2ND POET. Have you written any new poetry, Ragueneau?

[40]

CYRANO. '. . . who worships you . . .' [*He stops as he is about to sign it, gets up, and puts it in his pocket.*]

No need to sign it, though,
I shall give it to her.

RAGUENEAU [*to the* 2ND POET].

I've written a recipe
In verse.

3RD POET [*sitting at a plate of cream buns*].
Let's hear it, then!

4TH POET [*looking at a cake he has taken*].

It seems to me
This cake has its top knot back to front. [*He bites off the top.*]

IST POET. These spiced
Cakes make a hungry poet feel seduced
By their almond eyes! [*He grabs one.*]

2ND POET. We're listening.

3RD POET [*pinching a creamy cake*]. This puff
Has so much cream it's crying 'Hold, enough!'

2ND POET [*biting into the lyre of pastry*].
It's the first time I've found the Lyre sustaining!

RAGUENEAU [*striking an attitude*].
A Recipe in Verse . . .

2ND POET [*to the* 1ST, *nudging him*].
You're breakfasting?

IST POET. I'm dining!

RAGUENEAU.

HOW TO MAKE ALMOND TARTS
Beat, until it mercy begs,
  Two dozen eggs.
When the consistency's like silk
Add a cup of lemon juice,
  Then introduce
Two tablespoons of almond milk.

[41]

Layer the patty-cans to taste
        With custard paste:
Then, with clean hand, I implore,
Make a pattern shaped like wedges
        Round the edges.
Now the time has come to pour

In the pans your preparation
        With great elation
Insert in oven, medium heated,
Remove them when they're nicely browned.
        And what is found?
The tarts all ready to be eated!

THE POETS [*their mouths full*].
  Exquisite! Delicious!

A POET [*choking*].   Humph!

CYRANO [*to* RAGUENEAU].   You've seen
  How these greedy-guts, while lulled by your rhyme, have been
  Stuffing themselves?

RAGUENEAU [*quietly, with a smile*].
                  Yes, but I wouldn't harass them
  By seeming to notice: I think it might embarrass them.
  It gives me pleasure of a double kind
  To fill the belly and entertain the mind.

CYRANO [*patting him on the shoulder*].
  I'm very fond of you.
      [RAGUENEAU *rejoins his friends.* CYRANO *follows him with
      his eyes, then rather brusquely.*]
                  Here, Lise!
      [LISE, *in conversation with the* MUSKETEER, *starts, and comes
      down to* CYRANO.]

CYRANO.   This musketeer—
  Is he storming your defences?

LISE.   If any man dare
Threaten my virtue I destroy him with a look.

CYRANO. The all-conquering eye, according to my book,
Is the first to surrender.

LISE [*angry*].   But—

CYRANO.   I like Ragueneau,
And that, my madam Lise, is the reason
I won't let him be made a fool of.
    [*Raising his voice so that the* MUSKETEER *can hear.*]
                          A word in season!
    [*He bows to the* MUSKETEER *and goes to the door to look out,
after glancing at the clock. The* MUSKETEER *simply bows back.*]

LISE [*to the* MUSKETEER].
Well, you're a fine one! Why didn't you come to blows?
His nose was asking for it.

MUSKETEER.   Ah, yes . . . his nose . . .
    [*He moves away,* LISE *follows him.* CYRANO, *from the door,
makes signs to* RAGUENEAU *to get rid of the* POETS.]

CYRANO. Pst!

RAGUENEAU [*shepherding the* POETS *to a door, right.*]
            We'd find it quieter in there, you know—

CYRANO [*impatiently*].
Pst! Pst!

RAGUENEAU. —to read our poems.

1ST POET [*despairing, his mouth full*].
                    But the cakes!

2ND POET.   They can come, too!
    [*They all follow* RAGUENEAU *in procession, after sweeping all
the cakes off the tray.*]

CYRANO. If I see the faintest hope I'll produce my letter.
    [ROXANE, *masked, followed by the* DUENNA, *appears outside
the glass door.*]
Come in!— [*To the* DUENNA.] Can I have two words?

DUENNA.   Four would be better.

CYRANO. Do you like eating?

DUENNA.   I eat until I'm ill.

CYRANO. Good. Here's a sonnet—

DUENNA.   Oh?

CYRANO.   —which I'm going to fill
  With cakes.

DUENNA.   Oh!

CYRANO.   Are meringues at all an obsession?

DUENNA [with dignity].
  Monsieur, with cream they're practically my profession.

CYRANO. I'll put six into this sestina by Saint-Amant.
  Two macaroons in this. What more can you want?
  Now go and eat them out in the fresh air.

DUENNA.   What?

CYRANO [pushing her out].
  And don't come back until you have finished the lot!
  [He shuts the door after her, and comes back towards ROXANE,
  stopping, hat in hand, at a respectful distance.]

CYRANO. Well, here's a proud moment! You've remembered,
  eh,
  That I'm still breathing in my humble way?
  And come to tell me something—to tell me what?

ROXANE [taking off her mask].
  To thank you, first of all. Did you know, or not,
  The idiot you taught a lesson with your sword
  Last night, is the same man that a certain lord
  Who thinks he's in love with me—

CYRANO.   De Guiche?

ROXANE.   —is trying
  To force me to marry.

[44]

CYRANO.   We know what that's implying!
And so I fought (how could it be otherwise)
Not for my wretched nose, but your lovely eyes.

ROXANE. And also . . . I wanted . . . But first you must become
That boy again, that almost-brother, with whom
I used to play in the park down by the lake.

CYRANO. When you came each summer to visit Bergerac.

ROXANE. You made swords out of bullrushes—you remember,
surely?

CYRANO. And golden hair for your dolls out of the ripe barley.

ROXANE. Time was a game then.

CYRANO.   When unripe blackberries
Tasted like apples of the Hesperides.

ROXANE. You did whatever I told you to do then.

CYRANO. Roxane in pinafores, called Madeleine.

ROXANE. Was I pretty?

CYRANO.   Not bad.

ROXANE.   When you cut your hand
You would come running to me, and I'd pretend
To be mother, and talk to you very severely:
               [*She takes his hand.*]
'You haven't scratched yourself again? Well, really!'
               [*She pauses, taken aback by what she sees.*]
Oh, this is too much! Look here!
               [CYRANO *tries to take his hand away.*]

ROXANE.   No, let me see it.
Don't you ever grow up!—How did you do it?

CYRANO. Playing with grown-up boys at the Porte de Nesle.
     [ROXANE *sits and dips her handkerchief in a glass of water.*]

ROXANE. Show me!

CYRANO [*sitting beside her*].
               Motherly soul!

ROXANE.   Now tell me, tell

[45]

How many you fought with.

CYRANO.   Oh, a hundred or so.

ROXANE. The truth.

CYRANO.   Let's leave it. Suppose we turn to you
And what you dare not tell me?

ROXANE.   Now I dare.
I'm stronger for breathing again that country air,
And I dare now. I'm in love with someone.

CYRANO.   Ah!

ROXANE. Who doesn't know I am, moreover.

CYRANO.   Ah!

ROXANE. Not yet.

CYRANO.   Ah!

ROXANE.   But who soon will, if he doesn't.

CYRANO. Ah!

ROXANE.   A boy who loves me as though he mustn't,
Very shyly, from afar, not daring to speak.

CYRANO. Ah!

ROXANE.   Your hand's very hot; are you feverish?—This
week
I've begun to feel he was longing that I should know.

CYRANO. Ah!

ROXANE.   And oddly enough (isn't it curious, though?)
He's in your regiment.

CYRANO.   Ah!

ROXANE.   As a matter of fact
A cadet in your own platoon, to be exact.

CYRANO. Ah!

ROXANE. There's something exciting about him, I think. He's
young,
Courageous, handsome—

CYRANO [rising, very pale].   Handsome?

[46]

ROXANE.   Yes. What's wrong?

CYRANO. What? Nothing. Just—this graze. No matter.

ROXANE. In fact I love him. Even though so far
  I have simply seen him in the theatre.

CYRANO. Have you never spoken?

ROXANE.   Only with our eyes.

CYRANO. How do you know, then?

ROXANE.   I know. You can't disguise
  The heart's recognition; people talk.

CYRANO.   A cadet?

ROXANE. In the Guards.

CYRANO.   Called what?

ROXANE   Christian de Neuvillette.

CYRANO. What? *He's* not a cadet.

ROXANE.   Only since this morning.
  Under Captain de Castel-Jaloux.

CYRANO.   With so little warning
  The heart can melt! My poor child, you must take—

DUENNA [*opening the door*].
  I've finished the cakes, Monsieur de Bergerac!

CYRANO. Then read the verses on the wrapping paper!
              [*The* DUENNA *disappears.*]
  Dear girl, you know your heart is all for rapier-
  Wit and poetry. What on earth will you do
  If he proves to be a philistine yahoo?

ROXANE. He couldn't. His hair is as golden as Apollo.

CYRANO. But is his intellect? It doesn't follow.
  Suppose he is stupid.

ROXANE [*tapping her foot*]. Then I think I should die.

CYRANO. Was this what you came to tell me? And if so, why?

ROXANE. I've been so worried, ever since yesterday
  When I heard you all were Gascons in his company.

[47]

CYRANO. Who make it tough for any youth who's not,
And by influence gets into our pure-bred lot!
Is that what you have heard?

ROXANE.   Imagine how
Anxious I've been.

CYRANO [*between his teeth*].
                    With reason!

ROXANE.   However, now
Since yesterday, when you showed yourself so great
And unbeatable against that addle-pate
And all those brutes, I've thought—if this man would—
This man that everyone fears . . . Do you think you could?

CYRANO. All right, I'll take care of your little Baron.

ROXANE. Cousin! You really will see justice done?
I've always had such an affection for you.

CYRANO. Yes, yes.

ROXANE.   You will be his friend?

CYRANO.   I will. And now—

ROXANE. And not allow him to fight any duels?

CYRANO.   Not one.

ROXANE. Oh, I love you very much. Now I must fly.
    [*She quickly puts on her mask and veil, and adds absent-
    mindedly.*]
You haven't told me about last night's affray.
It must have been wonderful!—Do tell him to write.
                    [*She blows him a kiss.*]
Oh, I love you!

CYRANO.   Yes.

ROXANE.   A hundred men in the fight?
Well, goodbye for now. We are such tremendous friends!

CYRANO. Yes, yes.

[48]

ROXANE.   Make sure he writes.—A hundred men!
You must tell me about it, when we meet again.
A hundred! What courage!

CYRANO [*bowing*].   I've done better still since then.
[*She goes.* CYRANO *stands motionless, his eyes on the ground. A
silence. The door opens and* RAGUENEAU *looks in, followed by
the* POETS, CARBON DE CASTEL-JALOUX, *the* CADETS *and*
DE GUICHE.]

RAGUENEAU. May we come in?

CYRANO [*unmoving*].   Yes.
[RAGUENEAU *signs to his friends and they come in.* DE CASTEL-
JALOUX, *in uniform, makes gestures of surprise on seeing*
CYRANO.]

CARBON.   Here's the fellow!

CYRANO [*looking up*].   Captain?

CARBON [*delightedly*].
Hero! We know of it! Thirty of my men
Are here!

CYRANO [*recoiling*].
          But—

CARBON.   Come on, they want to lionize.

CYRANO. No!

CARBON.   They're across the road at the Golden Keys.

CYRANO. I—

CARBON [*yelling across the road*].
              The hero won't come. He's in a stubborn mood!

A VOICE [*outside*].
    Ah, *Sandious!*
[*Tumult outside. Noise of clanking swords and stamping.*]

CARBON [*rubbing his hands*].
              They're coming across the road!

CADETS [*entering*].
Milledious! Capedious! Mordious! Pocapedious!*

[49]

RAGUENEAU [*starting back*].
  Gentlemen, are you all Gascons?

CADETS.   All of us!

A CADET [*to* CYRANO].
  Bravo!

CYRANO. Baron!

ANOTHER [*shaking his hands*].
                        Vivat!

CYRANO.   Baron!

THIRD CADET.   Be kissed!

CYRANO. Baron!

SEVERAL CADETS. Be kissed by all of us!

CYRANO [*not knowing whom to reply to*].   Desist!

RAGUENEAU. Are all of you Barons?

CADETS.   All of us, all of us!

RAGUENEAU.   Really?

1ST CADET. You could build an obelisk out of our coronets,
  nearly!

LE BRET [*entering, hurrying to* CYRANO].
  I've been looking for you! All those who marched behind
    you
  Last night are rampaging through the streets to find you!

CYRANO. You haven't told them I'm here?

LE BRET [*rubbing his hands*].   Of course I have!

A TOWNSMAN [*entering, a crowd following*].
  Sir, the whole town is pouring here in a wave!
        [*Outside the street has filled with people.*]

LE BRET [*whispering and smiling to* CYRANO].
  What did Roxane—

CYRANO [*quickly*].   Be quiet!

[50]

CROWD [shouting offstage].   Cyrano! Prince of wits!
  [A CROWD rush into the shop, pushing one another. Acclamations.]

RAGUENEAU [standing on a table].
  My shop's invaded! They're smashing it all to bits!
  It's magnificent!

PEOPLE [crowding round CYRANO].
                    My friend! My friend! Hooray!

CYRANO. I seem to have made a few friends since yesterday!

LE BRET. Success!

A LITTLE MARQUIS [running, hands outstretched].
                    My dearest man!

CYRANO.   The rumour lied.

ANOTHER. Some ladies are waiting in their coach outside.
  I'll introduce you to them.

CYRANO.   Who could it be,
  I wonder, who presented *you* to *me*?

LE BRET [astonished].
  What's wrong with you?

CYRANO.   Be quiet!

A JOURNALIST [with notebook].   I'm most impressed.
  If I might record—

CYRANO.   No comment.

LE BRET [nudging him].   It's Theophraste
  Renaudot; he edits the Court Gazette.*

CYRANO. Somebody must.

LE BRET.   He's not a man to upset.
  It's a paper that can make or break your fame.

POET. I'm writing a pentacrostic on your name.

ANOTHER POET. Sir, I have a poem—

CYRANO.   I've had enough!
    [A movement in the crowd. DE GUICHE appears: also CUIGY,

[51]

BRISSAILLE *and the* OFFICERS *who went with* CYRANO *the night before.* CUIGY *comes quickly to* CYRANO.]

CUIGY. Monsieur de Guiche! He comes to you on behalf
  Of the Marshal—

DE GUICHE [*bowing to* CYRANO]. Who has deputed me to say
  He admires the originality of your display.
  On all men's lips your exploit has priority.

CROWD. Bravo!

CYRANO [*bowing*]. The marshal is a great authority.

DE GUICHE. He would never have believed it, had not these
  Gentlemen sworn they saw it—

CUIGY.   With our own eyes!

LE BRET [*aside to* CYRANO].
  What's up?

CYRANO.   Be quiet!

LE BRET.   You seem in distress, to me.

CYRANO. Distressed? In front of this lot?
          [*His moustache bristles. He throws out his chest.*]
                                          You shall see!

DE GUICHE [*to whom* CUIGY *has been whispering*].
  So your fame has already travelled through the land?
  You serve with the mad Gascons, I understand?

A CADET [*in a fierce voice*]. With *us*!

DE GUICHE [*looking at the* CADETS].
                    Ah! All those proud-looking gentlemen?
  So these are the famous—

CASTEL-JALOUX.   Cyrano!

CYRANO.   Captain?

CASTEL-JALOUX. All my company's here, I think. I wish
  You would introduce them to the Count de Guiche.

CYRANO [*introducing the Company*].
                    These are the Gascony cadets,
                    The men of de Castel-Jaloux;

[52]

Liars and layers of bets,
These are the Gascony cadets!
Bragging of crests and coronets,
And all the blood in them is blue!
These are the Gascony cadets,
The men of de Castel-Jaloux:

Hawk-eyed, with whiskers like a cat's,
Their long legs like a marabou,
They bully mobs with no regrets,
Hawk-eyed, with whiskers like a cat's,
They swagger in their ancient hats
With plumes to hide the holes from view,
Hawk-eyed, with whiskers like a cat's,
Their long legs like a marabou!

Here are the Gascony cadets
Who make the jealous go cuckoo!
Women, adorable coquettes,
Here are the Gascony cadets!
Old husbands don't know what to do:
Sound the trumpet, cry To-woo!
Here are the Gascony cadets
Who make the jealous go cuckoo!

Pity the enemy who gets
Between a Gascon and the view,
For when he settles ancient debts
He doesn't stop at empty threats
But storms across the parapets
With awful deeds of derring-do!
Here are the Gascony cadets,
The men of de Castel-Jaloux.

DE GUICHE [*lolling in a chair*].
    It's quite the thing to have a poet in train.
    I'll make you mine.

CYRANO.   Not you, nor any man!

[53]

DE GUICHE. Your brilliance last night much entertained
My uncle the Cardinal. And I intend
To speak to him about you.

LE BRET [*in* CYRANO's *ear*].   This is the day!

DE GUICHE. You've written, I imagine, a full-length play?

LE BRET [*in* CYRANO's *ear*].
You're going to have your 'Death of Agrippine'*
Performed at last!

DE GUICHE.   You would like it to be seen
By Richelieu? Send it to him.

CYRANO [*tempted and beguiled*].   I'd gladly send—

DE GUICHE. He's an expert critic. He'll probably amend
A line or two, not more.

CYRANO.   Out of the question!
It makes my blood run cold, the mere suggestion
Of changing a comma.

DE GUICHE.   But when he likes a line
His pleasure can pay well.

CYRANO.   Not as well as mine.
When I like what I've written, I'm so well repaid
I sing it all day long.

DE GUICHE.   You are very proud.

CYRANO. You've noticed that?
    [A CADET *enters with a string of old plumed hats, full of holes,
    spiked on his sword.*]

CADET.   Look, Cyrano! I say,
Look what we've bagged this morning on the quay—
The moulted feathers of those birds you chased away!

CARBON. Spolia opima!

ALL [*laughing*].   Ha! ha! ha!

CUIGY.   Whoever found the pay
For that bunch of thugs is regretting it today!

BRISSAILLE. Does anyone know who it was?

[54]

DE GUICHE.   Yes; it was I.
  Not work for *me* to do— [*The laughter stops.*]
                                I had to hire
  Others to punish that drunken versifier.
                          [*A constrained silence.*]

CADET [*whispering to* CYRANO, *indicating the hats on his sword*].
  What shall we do with these? They're greasy. Make them
  Into a stew?

CYRANO [*taking the sword and with a salute dropping them at* DE
    GUICHE'*s feet.*]
                    Perhaps, sir, you will take them
  Back to your friends?

DE GUICHE [*rising, sharply*]. Call my chair—do you hear?
  I'm leaving. [*To* CYRANO, *passionately.*] As for you!

A VOICE [*calling in the street*].   The Count de Guiche's chair!

DE GUICHE [*controlled, smiling*].
  Have you read *Don Quixote*?

CYRANO.   With great delight.
  I take my hat off to that old fly-by-night.

DE GUICHE. I suggest you study—

PORTER [*at the door*].   Your chair, my lord!

DE GUICHE.   —I mean
  The passage about the windmills.

CYRANO.   Chapter Thirteen.*

DE GUICHE. When you make war on windmills you may
    find—

CYRANO. I'm tilting at men who veer with every wind?

DE GUICHE. That those mill-sails will thrash their mighty spars
    And throw you in the mud.

CYRANO.   Or up among the stars!
    [DE GUICHE *goes, followed by the other* LORDS *whispering
    together.* LE BRET *goes to the door with them. The* CROWD
    disperses.]

[55]

CYRANO [*giving mocking bows to those who go without daring to salute him*].

Gentlemen . . . Gentlemen . . .

LE BRET [*returning, in despair*].   Here's a fine old mess!

CYRANO. Oh, you! Stop grumbling!

LE BRET.   Well, you must confess
This habit of ruining every chance you get
Is becoming too much.

CYRANO.   I like to exaggerate.

LE BRET. Can't you see? Fame and fortune would accrue
If you'd only behave!

CYRANO.   What would you have me do?
Search out some powerful patronage, and be
Like crawling ivy clinging to a tree?
No thank you. Dedicate, like all the others,
Verses to plutocrats, while caution smothers
Whatever might offend my lord and master?
No thank you. Kneel until my knee-caps fester,
Bend my back until I crack my spine,
And scratch another's back if he'll scratch mine?
No thank you. Dining out to curry favour,
Meeting the influential till I slaver,
Suiting my style to what the critics want
With slavish copy of the latest cant?
No thanks! Ready to jump through any hoop
To be the great man of a little group?
Be blown off course, with madrigals for sails,
By the old women sighing through their veils?
Labouring to write a line of such good breeding
Its only fault is—that it's not worth reading?
To ingratiate myself, abject with fear,
And fawn and flatter to avoid a sneer?
No thanks, no thanks, no thanks! But . . . just to sing,
Dream, laugh, and take my tilt of wing,
To cock a snook whenever I shall choose,

To fight for 'yes' and 'no', come win or lose,
To travel without thought of fame or fortune
Wherever I care to go to under the moon!
Never to write a line that hasn't come
Directly from my heart: and so, with some
Modesty, to tell myself: 'My boy,
Be satisfied with a flower, a fruit, the joy
Of a single leaf, so long as it was grown
In your own garden. Then, if success is won
By any chance, you have nothing to render to
A hollow Caesar: the merit belongs to you.'
In short, I won't be a parasite; I'll be
My own intention, stand alone and free,
And suit my voice to what my own eyes see!

LE BRET. Then be alone; but not against all the earth.
Why the devil do you think it's worth
Always making enemies everywhere?

CYRANO. After watching you grin from ear to ear
To keep so many friends, I thought I should
Economize on smiling, if I could,
And cry 'That's one more enemy to the good!'

LE BRET. It's lunacy!

CYRANO.   Well, it's my only vice.
I find displeasing people is rather nice.
I love being hated. God! how my spirits rise
Under a cannonade of glaring eyes!
—Your circle of friends, so flattering to the face,
Are like a collar of Italian lace,
More comfortable, but less dignified.
Your head can loll at will from side to side,
Unchafed by any certainty of mind.
The kindness that it gives is not my kind.
Hate, with its rigid gofering and wire
Gives me the frame to hold my head up higher,

[57]

Exactly as a Spanish ruff will do.
Hate makes a pillory, but a halo, too!

LE BRET [*after a silence, taking his arm*].
  You can fly that flag of bitter pride above you,
  But what's down in your heart? She doesn't love you.

CYRANO [*quickly*]. Be quiet!
    [CHRISTIAN *has just entered and mingled with the* CADETS *who
    don't speak to him; he has seated himself at a table where* LISE
    serves him.]

A CADET [*at another table, glass in hand*].
                        Cyrano! [CYRANO *turns.*] The story!

CYRANO.   In good time.

THE CADET [*rising*]. The story of the fight! It'll be a prime
  Example for the shy apprentice here.

CHRISTIAN [*looking up*]. Apprentice?

ANOTHER CADET.   Yes, you feeble Northerner!

CHRISTIAN. Feeble?

IST CADET [*mockingly*]. A word: there's something we don't
    dare
  To mention here, it simply isn't done,
  No more than you'd say 'Rope' to a hanged man's son.

CHRISTIAN. What is it?

ANOTHER CADET.   Observe!
    [*He taps three times on his nose mysteriously.*]
                        Do you understand?

CHRISTIAN. You mean the—

ANOTHER CADET.   Ssh!—Don't breathe the word,
    it's banned!
    [*Pointing to where* CYRANO *is talking to* LE BRET.]
  Or else you'll have to deal with—him over there.

ANOTHER [*who has come up noiselessly to sit on the table*].
  He killed two men who were suffering from catarrh

[58]

Because they spoke through their noses.

ANOTHER.   If you don't
Want to die before your time, you won't
Make cartilagenous references out loud.

ANOTHER. Pull out your handkerchief and you draw your
shroud!
    [*Silence. All with crossed arms look at* CHRISTIAN. *He rises
    and goes across to* CARBON DE CASTEL-JALOUX *who is
    talking to an* OFFICER.]

CHRISTIAN. Captain!

CARBON [*turning and looking him up and down*].
                    Well, sir?

CHRISTIAN.   What is it best to do
When you find these Southerners taking it out on you?

CARBON. Prove to them that a Northerner has nerve.
                    [*He turns his back on him.*]

CHRISTIAN. Thank you.

1ST CADET [*to* CYRANO]. Now the story! We all deserve
To hear your story!

ALL.   Your story!

CYRANO [*coming down to them*].   My story? Well,
I went alone to meet these men. The pale
Moon was shining, like a round watch-face,
Until a cloud came, and snapped shut the case.
Then all around was dark as Erebus.
God's truth, I couldn't see further—

CHRISTIAN.   —than your nose.
    [*Silence. Everyone slowly gets up, looking at* CYRANO *in terror.*
    CYRANO *has stopped, dumbfounded. Pause.*]

CYRANO. Who's that man?

A CADET [*nervously*].   He came this morning.

[59]

CYRANO [taking a step towards CHRISTIAN].   Came
  This morning?

CARBON.   Yes, this morning: and his name
  Is the Baron de Neuvill . . .

CYRANO [interrupting].   All right!
    [He changes colour, makes to attack CHRISTIAN.]
                                               I . . .
    [Then controlling himself.]   Very well
  As I was saying— [With a burst of rage.]
                                Good God!
    [Calming down.]   —It was dark as hell.
    [Astonishment. The CADETS sit down again, staring at
    CYRANO.]
  I walked on, thinking 'For a drunkard's sake
  I'm offending a great noble who could break—'

CHRISTIAN. Your nose.
                    [All rise. CHRISTIAN balances on his chair.]

CYRANO [in a choked voice]. My reputation. In this way
  I antagonized someone who could make me pay—

CHRISTIAN. —through the nose.

CYRANO.   —Dearly for it. Still,
  A Gascon has to settle Duty's bill,
  So on I marched. And then out of the dark,
  What did I see?

CHRISTIAN.   Who knows?

CYRANO.   —they missed their mark
  With a sword-thrust. I swung to meet my foes,
  And suddenly came—

CHRISTIAN.   —nose to nose . . .

CYRANO [bounding towards him].   God's teeth!
    [The CADETS leap up to see, but when he is close to CHRISTIAN
    he controls himself and continues.]
  Face to face with a hundred toughs whose breath—

CHRISTIAN. Was offensive to the nostrils . . .

[60]

CYRANO [*white, but smiling*].   —stank of wine,
    Onions and turpentine. I charged, and ran
    Two of them through: another in the midriff—
    A fourth comes at me: Paf! and I parry—

CHRISTIAN.   Pif!

CYRANO [*bursting out*].
    Christ! Get out of here, fast as you can!
        [*All the* CADETS *run towards the door.*]

1ST CADET. The tiger wakes!

CYRANO.   Leave me alone with this man!

2ND CADET. He'll make mincemeat of him!

RAGUENEAU.   Mincemeat?

ANOTHER CADET.   On one of your plates!

RAGUENEAU. I've gone as limp as one of my serviettes!

CARBON. Come on.

ANOTHER CADET.   It kills me to think of the poor chap's fate!

ANOTHER [*shutting the door right*].
    It's something too horrible to contemplate!
        [*All have gone out by different doors, some by the staircase.*
        CYRANO *and* CHRISTIAN *are left face to face, looking at one*
        another for a moment.]

CYRANO. Suppose we shake hands?

CHRISTIAN.   Sir?

CYRANO.   I like your pluck.

CHRISTIAN. But—

CYRANO.   Very much. I expected you to crack.

CHRISTIAN. You mean—?

CYRANO.   Come on. I'm her brother, don't forget.

CHRISTIAN. Whose?

CYRANO.   Why, hers—Roxane's.

CHRISTIAN.   O God! you're not?

CYRANO. Well, her fraternal cousin.

[61]

CHRISTIAN. Did she say—?

CYRANO. Everything.

CHRISTIAN. Does she love me?

CYRANO. She may, she may

CHRISTIAN [*taking his hands*].
I'm happy to know you, sir!

CYRANO. That's an event
Remarkable for its change of sentiment.

CHRISTIAN. Forgive me.

CYRANO [*looking at him, hand on shoulder*].
It's quite true what she said: the wretch
Is handsome.

CHRISTIAN. Sir, I admire you very much.

CYRANO. How about all those noses?

CHRISTIAN. I take them back.

CYRANO. Roxane's expecting to hear from you.

CHRISTIAN. Oh, heck!

CYRANO. Why?

CHRISTIAN. Because I'm lost if I say a word.

CYRANO. How's that?

CHRISTIAN. I'm so slow-witted I feel absurd.

CYRANO. It takes brains to know that you haven't any.
And your clash with me was moderately funny.

CHRISTIAN. I can cope all right with mess-room banter. It's
When I'm faced with a woman I go to bits.
Their eyes encourage me when I'm walking by them.

CYRANO. But not their hearts when you make a halt and try
them?

CHRISTIAN. No, I'm one of those men—I don't know why—
So tongue-tied in love I sometimes wish I could die.

CYRANO. While I could speak it all, on the other hand,
  If only my face were more expertly planned.

CHRISTIAN. Oh, to be able to say things with some grace!

CYRANO. To be a young cadet with a pretty face!

CHRISTIAN. To a woman like Roxane I'm bound to be
  A terrible let-down.

CYRANO [*studying* CHRISTIAN]. If the soul in me
  Could have a fitting interpreter!

CHRISTIAN [*in despair*].   O God,
  I need eloquence!

CYRANO.   Yes, that's understood.
  I'll lend you mine, if, in return, you lend
  To me what you possess, that cunning blend
  Of youth and charm, so acceptable to Venus.
  We'd make a romantic hero, you know, between us.

CHRISTIAN. What?

CYRANO.   Do you think you could learn by heart
  each day
  The words I taught you?

CHRISTIAN.   What are you trying to say?

CYRANO. Suppose we unite to be the best of men?
  Roxane wouldn't be disillusioned then,
  With my articulate spirit shining out
  Through your fine façade.

CHRISTIAN.   But—

CYRANO.   Christian, why not?
  All you need is a tongue, and I'll provide it.
  How do you know it won't work until you've tried it?

CHRISTIAN. I'd be terrified!

CYRANO.   Maybe, but aren't you now?—
  Scared of approaching her?—My words, and you
  To say them—*then*! Christian, don't you see?
  The perfect collaboration! Will you agree?

[63]

CHRISTIAN. Your eyes are shining!

CYRANO.   Will you?

CHRISTIAN.   Would it give you pleasure?

CYRANO [*excitedly*].

　Oh, it w'd—[*Recollecting himself.*]
　　　　　　Certainly, in some measure.
　It's a situation tempting to a poet,
　Like speaking through a mask. Well? Shall we do it?
　I'll be your eloquence and you my beauty.

CHRISTIAN. This letter she's expecting—in all duty
　I'll never be able—

CYRANO [*producing one from his pocket*].
　　　　　　　　Hey presto, here it is!

CHRISTIAN. What?

CYRANO.   It's all here, except for the address.

CHRISTIAN. I—

CYRANO.   You can send it with an easy mind.
　It's something of a masterpiece of its kind.

CHRISTIAN. Have you—?

CYRANO.   Several more where this came from.
　We poets have our pockets crammed with them—
　Passionate letters to a phantom, some ideal one.
　Far better you should use it on a real one.
　Being insincere, it's all the more affecting.

CHRISTIAN. But surely a word or two will need correcting?
　Will it suit Roxane?

CYRANO.   Fit her like a glove.

CHRISTIAN. But—

CYRANO.   Don't you know the credulity of love?
　She will believe—after she has admired it—
　That she, in every phrase and word, inspired it!

CHRISTIAN [*embracing* CYRANO].
　My friend!

[64]

A CADET [*half opening the door*].
    Not a sound. A silence like the grave.
 I daren't go in. [*He puts his head in.*]
     What?
  [*All the* CADETS *come in and see* CYRANO *and* CHRISTIAN
  embracing.]

CADETS.   Oh!

A CADET.   I don't believe it!

CARBON. The devil's a saint! What Christian could go further?
 Struck on one nostril he has turned the other!

MUSKETEER. Can we all mention his nose now, do you think?
      [*Sniffing ostentatiously.*]
 Do you smell anything, Lise? A frightful stink!
    [*Going to* CYRANO *and staring at his nose.*]
 What can it be? *You* have the nose to discover—
 Isn't this smell enough to—

CYRANO [*sending him flying*]. Knock you over?
  [*General delight. The* CADETS *have found the old* CYRANO
  again. They turn somersaults.]

CURTAIN

ACT THREE

A small square in the old Marais. On the right ROXANE's *house.
Window and balcony over the door. A bench in front. On the left
another house. The* DUENNA *is sitting on the bench. The window of*
ROXANE's *balcony is wide open.* RAGUENEAU *is standing near
the door in a sort of livery. He has just finished relating something to
the* DUENNA *and is wiping his eyes.*

RAGUENEAU. —And then she went off with a musketeer.
  Alone and ruined, I hanged myself in despair.
  Monsieur de Bergerac came and cut me down.
  And got me this job with his cousin in the town.

DUENNA. But what ruined you?

RAGUENEAU.   Well! Lise, you see,
  Was devoted to soldiers, and poets were welcome to me.
  So Mars finished off all the cakes left by Apollo.
  With that going on, ruin was bound to follow.

DUENNA [*calling up to the window*].
  Roxane, are you ready? We're keeping them waiting.

VOICE OF ROXANE.   Yes,
  I'll just get my cloak.

DUENNA [*to* RAGUENEAU]. They're all at Clomire's house.
  She likes to be thought an artistic leader of fashion.
  Someone is giving a talk on the Tender Passion.*

RAGUENEAU. On the Tender—?

DUENNA.   Passion!
          [*Calling up to the window.*]
                        Roxane, we shall be late
  For that lecture on how to be tenderly passionate!

[66]

VOICE OF ROXANE. I'm coming!
[*The sound of stringed instruments approaching.*]

VOICE OFF. La, la, la, la!

DUENNA [*surprised*]. Are they going to sing to us?

CYRANO [*entering with* PAGES *carrying lutes*].
I told you that was a minim, you minimal ass!
Let's try again. La! La! La!

ROXANE [*appearing on the balcony*]. Is it you?

CYRANO [*singing*]. I, Cyrano, serenader of all that's true,
Saluting the lily and rose and the light of your hair!

DUENNA. And why, may we ask, are these two infant prodigies
here?

CYRANO. I won them—in a wager with D'Assoucy,
Over a point of grammar. 'All right,' said he,
Pointing to these two gangling strummers of song,
'I'll bet you a day's music that you're wrong.'
He lost. Now I can't do anything, or say it,
But these two plucking children try to play it.
This will go on till the sun comes up again.
It was pleasant at first, but I'm starting to feel the strain.
[*To the* PAGES.]
Skip! You have my permission to play a pavane
To Montfleury! [*To the* DUENNA.] I came here to ask
Roxane,
As I do every night— [*To the* PAGES.] Make it long, and
play out of tune!—
[*To the* DUENNA.]
—if her soul's idol is totally immune
To human failings.

ROXANE [*coming from the house*]. How handsome he is, and how
Witty! I love him!

CYRANO. Is Christian *witty* now?

ROXANE. My dear, even more than you are.

CYRANO. I accept.

[67]

ROXANE. No one can rival him—he is so adept
At those charming nothings that contain so much.
Though, strangely, he sometimes seems to lose his touch.
But then there comes another burst of flame!

CYRANO [*incredulous*].
It can't be true!

ROXANE. Oh, you men are all the same.
You think a handsome man can't have intellect!

CYRANO. Does he really speak of love with such effect?

ROXANE. It's more than speech: a harvest of gallantries.

CYRANO. And writes just as well?

ROXANE. Even better. Listen to this:
'The more you steal from my heart, the more my heart
contains.'
[*Triumphantly.*] Well?

CYRANO. Pooh!

ROXANE. And this:
'Since I must have a heart, to beat and break,
And you have mine, your heart I will have to take!'

CYRANO. First he has too much, then too little. Slate me,
How much heart does he want?

ROXANE. You infuriate me!
It's jealousy—

CYRANO [*startled*]. What?

ROXANE. —of writing you can't compete with.
Real tenderness, such as this, you seldom meet with:
'All that my heart would say to you is this:
My pen brushes the paper like a kiss—
Then read this letter, lady, with your lips.'

CYRANO [*pleased, in spite of himself*].
Not bad! . . . I mean . . . Apart from a few slips.

ROXANE. And then again—

CYRANO. You know these letters by heart?

ROXANE. Every one!

CYRANO. Well, if flattery is an art—

ROXANE. He's a master!

CYRANO [*modestly*]. A master?

ROXANE. A master!

CYRANO. Just as you say.

DUENNA [*coming down quickly*].
Here's Monsieur de Guiche!
[*Pushing* CYRANO *towards the house.*]
You'd better get out of the way!
It might put him on to the scent if he finds you here.

ROXANE. Of my secret, yes. I've every reason to fear.
He's in love with me, and so powerful, he could put
An end to it all!

CYRANO [*going in*]. I go!

ROXANE [*curtseying as* DE GUICHE *enters*].
We were just going out.

DE GUICHE. I came to say goodbye.

ROXANE. Are you going away?

DE GUICHE. To the battlefield.

ROXANE. Oh, when?

DE GUICHE. Why, now, today.
We're besieging Arras.

ROXANE. Arras?

DE GUICHE. But I see
My going doesn't concern you.

ROXANE [*being civil*]. Certainly.

DE GUICHE. It breaks my heart. When shall I see you again?
I've been made commanding officer.

ROXANE. Well done.

DE GUICHE. Of the Guards regiment.

ROXANE. The Guards?

DE GUICHE.   The one
  That your vainglorious cousin is serving in.
  Now I can get my own back on him at last.

ROXANE. The Guards go to Arras?

DE GUICHE.   Yes, the die is cast.

ROXANE [*sinking on to the bench, aside*].
  Christian!

DE GUICHE. What's the matter?

ROXANE.   I'm in despair,
  To know that someone I care for goes to war!

DE GUICHE [*surprised and delighted*].
  That is the first time you have said anything
  So kind, and the day I'm leaving!

ROXANE [*recovering and fanning herself*]. So you mean to bring
  My cousin to his knees?

DE GUICHE.   Are you on his side?

ROXANE. Quite the reverse, however hard I tried.

DE GUICHE. Do you see him?

ROXANE.   Very seldom.

DE GUICHE.   He's often about
  With this Neu—villen?—viller?—anyway, a cadet.

ROXANE. Tall?

DE GUICHE.   Fair.

ROXANE.   Carroty.

DE GUICHE.   Handsome.

ROXANE.   So-so.

DE GUICHE. But a fool.

ROXANE.   He looks it—Now what I want to know
  Is how you will take your revenge on Cyrano?
  Put him in the firing-line, which he adores?
  If so, I have a better idea than yours.

DE GUICHE. Which is?

[70]

ROXANE. If you left him here with his dear cadets
For the whole of the war, you would strangle him with
regrets.
It's the one way you could make him mad with anger.
If you want to punish him, keep him out of danger.

DE GUICHE. A woman! Trust a woman to find the neat
Way to retaliate!

ROXANE. It would make him eat
His heart out, his friends too, not to be in battle:
And you would have your revenge!

DE GUICHE. So you love me a little?
Can I believe that taking my side in this
Is a proof of love?

ROXANE. Of love? I think it is.

DE GUICHE [*showing some sealed papers*].
These are the marching-orders. They must be got
To each company immediately—but . . . [*He detaches one.*]
This one for the cadets—won't go tonight.
So much for Cyrano's craving for a fight!
—So even you can be cunning?

ROXANE. Now and then.

DE GUICHE. I'm dazzled! This evening—yes, I know it's when
I should have left—but how can I do that
Just when I hear your heart begin to beat? . . .
Listen. You know the monastery down the road
Run by the Capucins? They don't allow
The laity inside, but I know how
To persuade the good monks. Their habits have wide
Sleeves, you know, in which a man can hide.
—Everyone will suppose me gone. But I
Can mask myself and come to you secretly.
Let me postpone my going one more night.

ROXANE. If you're discovered, your good name—

DE GUICHE. Oh, that!

ROXANE. What about the siege of Arras?

DE GUICHE.   Yes, it's a pity,
But let me stay.

ROXANE.   No!

DE GUICHE.   Please!

ROXANE [*tenderly*].   No, it's my duty
To protect you.

DE GUICHE.   To protect me?

ROXANE [*aside*].   Christian stays.
[*Aloud.*] I want you to be heroic, —Antoine!

DE GUICHE.   Praise
Be, you've called me Antoine! And you love, you would
say—

ROXANE. Someone who troubles my heart.

DE GUICHE [*in a transport of joy*].   I'm on my way!
                [*He kisses her hand.*]
Does it put your mind at rest?

ROXANE.   Oh, yes, my dear!
        [*Exit* DE GUICHE. *The* DUENNA *comes down.*]

DUENNA [*with a mock curtsey*].
Oh, yes, my dear!

ROXANE [*to the* DUENNA]. Don't give me away! Will you swear?
Cyrano would never forgive me for stealing his war.
                [*She calls towards the house.*]
Cousin!
                [CYRANO *enters.*]
        We're going to Clomire's, to hear the talk
Alcandre is giving.

DUENNA.   Too late. It's a wasted walk.

CYRANO [*to* ROXANE].
Enjoy the sermon.

DUENNA [*ecstatically, at Clomire's door*].
                The dear little knocker's been wrapped

[72]

In swaddling clothes, to make sure it won't interrupt!
[*She knocks very gently at the door.*]

ROXANE [*seeing the door is open*].
We can go in. [*To* CYRANO.] If Christian comes, as I know
He will, ask him to wait.

CYRANO [*quickly*].   Just before you go—
[*She comes back.*]
Have you thought what topic you mean to discuss with him?
As you usually do.

ROXANE.   What topic?

CYRANO.   This evening's whim.

ROXANE. You'll keep silent about it?

CYRANO.   As if I were dead.

ROXANE. No topic at all. I shall say: 'I give you your head.
Improvise. Play on love with your ravishing touch.'

CYRANO [*smiling*].
Good.

ROXANE [*with finger on lips*].
        Shsh!

CYRANO.   Shsh!

ROXANE   Not a word!
[*She goes in and shuts the door.*]

CYRANO [*once the door is shut*].   Thanks very much!
[*The door reopens and* ROXANE *puts her head out.*]

ROXANE. In case he rehearses it!

CYRANO.   Heaven forbid it!

BOTH [*together*].   Shsh!
[*The door shuts.*]

CYRANO [*calling* CHRISTIAN, *who enters*].
Christian! I know what she wants. We must get ready.
This is the time to cover yourself with glory.
There's not a minute to lose. We'd better go
Back to my house and start the lesson—

[73]

CHRISTIAN. No!

CYRANO. Why not?

CHRISTIAN. I'll wait for Roxane.

CYRANO. Now have some sense!
Come on, let's—

CHRISTIAN. No! I'm sick of all this pretence!
My thoughts, my letters—nothing but dissembling.
And all the time I play the part I'm trembling.
It was all very well to begin with. But now that I know
She loves me, —thanks, I can handle my own plough.

CYRANO. Hey!

CHRISTIAN. And what makes you think that I can't do it?
I'm not an utter fool, and I mean to show it.
Your lessons have been useful, I admit they have,
But now I can speak for myself—and heaven's above!
I know jolly well how to put my arms around her! . . .
[Noticing ROXANE coming out of Clomire's house.]
She's here! Cyrano, don't leave me! I shall founder!

CYRANO. Sink in your own way, dear fellow.
[He disappears behind the garden wall.]

ROXANE [taking leave of friends]. Baptiste!
Alcandre! . . .

DUENNA. I was furious that we missed
The talk on the Tender Passion!
[She goes into ROXANE's house.]

ROXANE [still taking leave]. Goodbye, goodnight,
Goodnight!
[All bow to ROXANE and to each other, and go their separate
ways. ROXANE suddenly sees CHRISTIAN.]

ROXANE. Is that you, Christian? . . . [She comes to him.]
Let us enjoy
The peace of the evening. No one passing by.
The air so soft, the first stars glistening.
Let us sit down. Now talk. I'm listening.

[74]

CHRISTIAN [*beside her on the bench*].
  I love you.

ROXANE [*her eyes closed*].
            Go on.

CHRISTIAN.   I love you.

ROXANE.   We have the theme,
  Now play the variations.

CHRISTIAN.   I love—

ROXANE.   The same
  As ever?

CHRISTIAN. I love you very much.

ROXANE.   And so?

CHRISTIAN. I'd be very glad if you could love me, too.
  Tell me, Roxane, that you love me!

ROXANE [*pouting*].   You give me the skim
  Of the milk when I was hoping for the cream.
  How do you love me?

CHRISTIAN.   Why, a very great deal.

ROXANE. Oh. Do the very great sentiments congeal?

CHRISTIAN. May I kiss your throat?

ROXANE.   Christian!

CHRISTIAN.   I love you!

ROXANE [*half-rising*].   Once more you—

CHRISTIAN [*eagerly, detaining her*].
  No, I don't love you!

ROXANE [*sitting again*].   A change, at least.

CHRISTIAN.   I adore you!

ROXANE [*rising and moving away*].
  Oh!

CHRISTIAN. I'm a clot!

ROXANE [*dryly*].   Which gives me the same pain
  As if, instead of handsome, you were plain.

CHRISTIAN. But—

ROXANE. So hurry and set the tide of eloquence flowing!

CHRISTIAN. I—

ROXANE. Love me. I know. Goodnight.
[*She goes towards the house.*]

CHRISTIAN. Oh, you're not going?
I wanted to say—

ROXANE [*opening the door*]. How much you loved me, yes.
No! Go away!

CHRISTIAN. But—
[*She shuts the door in his face.*]

CYRANO [*who has just entered unseen*].
That was a great success.

CHRISTIAN. Help me!

CYRANO. Oh, no!

CHRISTIAN. I shall die if I can't at once
Get myself back into her good graces!

CYRANO. Dunce,
How the hell do you think I can teach you on the spot?

CHRISTIAN [*seizing his arm*].
Look, there she is!

CYRANO [*moved*]. Her window!

CHRISTIAN. I'll die!

CYRANO. Or not.
But keep your voice down.

CHRISTIAN. I'll die!

CYRANO. It's a dark night.

CHRISTIAN. What of it?

CYRANO. There might be a way—I only said 'might'.
You don't deserve it, but still. Stand over here,
You misery, in front of the window—there!
I'll prompt you from the shadows.

[76]

CHRISTIAN. I'm afraid—

CYRANO. Keep quiet!

THE PAGES [*appearing with their lutes*].
Sir!

CYRANO. Hush!

1ST PAGE [*in a whisper*]. We've finished the serenade
To Montfleury.

CYRANO [*quickly, quietly*].
Go to each end of the street,
And if you hear the sound of anyone's feet,
Anyone who seems to be coming this way,
Play a tune.

2ND PAGE. What tune do you want us to play?

CYRANO. Spritely for a woman, sad if it's a man.
[*The* PAGES *go.*]

CYRANO [*to* CHRISTIAN].
Now call!

CHRISTIAN. Roxane!

CYRANO [*picking up gravel and throwing*].
Wait a minute—we'll try a stone!

ROXANE [*half-opening the window*].
Who is calling?

CHRISTIAN. I.

ROXANE. What 'I'?

CHRISTIAN. It's Christian.

ROXANE [*disdainfully*].
Oh, you!

CHRISTIAN. I want to talk to you again.

CYRANO [*under the balcony, to* CHRISTIAN].
You're doing well. Put feeling into what you say.

ROXANE. No. You talk too stupidly. Go away.

CHRISTIAN. Please listen!

[77]

ROXANE. You don't love me any more.

CHRISTIAN [*prompted by* CYRANO].
You say—great God!—not any more, you say—
When my love grows stronger—every hour of the day!

ROXANE [*who was about to shut the window*].
That's rather better.

CHRISTIAN. Growing—how to restrain it?—
Like a child—the cradling heart cannot contain it!

ROXANE. Better still! But surely the troublesome brat
Should have been stifled at birth?

CHRISTIAN. Oh, I tried that—
I tried that—without the least success.
Even at birth—he was a Hercules.

ROXANE. Better and better.

CHRISTIAN. With a strength so stout—
He could strangle—those twin serpents, Pride—and Doubt.

ROXANE [*leaning over the balcony*].
Well said! But why do you talk with so many stops?
Does your imagination flow in drops?

CYRANO [*changing places with* CHRISTIAN].*
Come on! This is getting too difficult!

ROXANE. Tonight
Your words are so halting. Why?

CYRANO. In this dim light
They have to grope through shadows to your ear.

ROXANE. But mine have no trouble.

CYRANO. Their target is so clear
No wonder. My heart's capacious to receive them;
Your ears are small, and careless to believe them.
Beside, yours are descending, mine must climb;
Falling is swift, but rising takes up time.

ROXANE. They are flying more easily now.

[78]

CYRANO.   As well they may,
  Finding their wings.

ROXANE.   I feel so far away.

CYRANO. And so you are—and from a place so high
  Drop one hard word on my heart and I should die!

ROXANE [*with a movement*].
  I'll come down.

CYRANO [*quickly*]. No!

ROXANE.   Climb up on the bench, then.

CYRANO.   No!

ROXANE. Why not?

CYRANO.   Don't let this perfect moment go
  Which comes by chance, this heaven-sent power, I mean,
  To talk together, untroubled, and unseen.

ROXANE. Unseen?

CYRANO.   It's marvellous to be half lost,
  Just a darkness moving; and you a ghost
  In your white summer dress—merely the light
  Conversing with a shadow in the night.
  How much it means to me you can never know.
  If only I could express it—

ROXANE.   But you do.

CYRANO. Words never came so straight from my heart before.

ROXANE. Why not?

CYRANO.   Always before, when I saw you clear,
  I was half-drunk with looking. Now I seem
  To be talking with you for the first time.

ROXANE. Yes, your voice has a new sound.

CYRANO.   Because the night
  Protects me, I can dare to claim a right
  To be myself at last, and dare . . . What have I said?—
  I don't know . . . Forgive me . . . I seem to have strayed
  Into a new world—

[79]

ROXANE.   New?

CYRANO.   —without the fear
Of the mockery that I find so hard to bear.

ROXANE. Mockery of what?

CYRANO.   Of my reality.
I keep my feelings covered up with wit
For decency's sake. I reach above my head
For a star, and hastily pick a flower instead
Not to be thought ridiculous.

ROXANE.   A flower
Is well worth picking.

CYRANO.   I scorn it now!

ROXANE.   A power
Is in you tonight I never heard before.

CYRANO. All the flirting candles of life are out
And we breathe pure air. This is what life's about:
Not lifting the frail glass to a cautious lip,
But slaking our heartfelt thirst by drinking deep.

ROXANE. And wit?

CYRANO.   To catch your ear it could be used,
But now with wit the night would be abused.
Look up at the stars—the great distances there
Strip us of all our pretences. And I fear
Our exquisite art of living only kills
True feeling, and all the waiting miracles.
Make life a pastime, life passes us by,
And dying to live we only live to die.

ROXANE. But the wit?

CYRANO.   In love it's hateful! Who would wish
To turn passion into a fencing-match?
There comes an inevitable moment in a lifetime—
And I pity those to whom it has never come—
When a man achieves a love of such high faith
That every playful word is like a death.

[80]

ROXANE. And if it has come, this moment, to us both,
  With what words will you say it?

CYRANO.   All of them, all words, all
  The words my heart knows, like flowers hurled
  In wild disorder over a summer world.
  I love, I am choked with love, I love, I rave
  With love, more love there cannot be, it brims
  And overflows, a cataract of dreams.
  Your name rings like a sheep-bell in my heart,
  I tremble and it sounds—Roxane! No part
  Of any day is forgotten if you were there:
  I know that on the tenth of May last year
  You had altered a little the way you wore your hair!
  To me your hair is the heart of light. And often,
  As it is when we have stared too long at the sun
  Everywhere we look is flecked with red,
  I turn away from watching you, and tread
  A landscape dancing with your fire.

ROXANE [*her voice troubled*].   Indeed
  This is love.

CYRANO.   This certainly is love,
  This merciless power invading me from above,
  Certainly love—with all its raging sadness;
  Love, indeed, and yet not self-love's madness.
  To guard your happiness I'd destroy my own
  (Though both deed and reason were never known),
  If sometimes, however far away, I thought you
  Laughed because of the happiness I had brought you.
  —Each look you give me, a new virtue is born,
  A greater courage. Do you begin to discern,
  To understand now? Are you recognizing?
  And feel, do you, my spirit like incense rising
  Up through the dark? This night is far too dear
  Ever to end. I speak to you—you hear!
  I and you! Hope never ran so high,

[81]

And nothing now remains except to die!
Has the thought made you tremble as one who grieves?
For you *do* tremble, a leaf among the leaves.
I can feel the gentle trembling of your hand
Shaking the jasmine branches where I stand!
[*He kisses the hanging spray of jasmine.*]

ROXANE. Yes, I am trembling, and weeping. I am yours.
I am spellbound.

CYRANO.　　　　Then death can take its course!
I, the besotted, have accomplished this!
I have only one more thing to ask—

CHRISTIAN [*under the balcony*].　　　A kiss!

ROXANE [*drawing back*].
What?

CYRANO. Oh!

ROXANE.　　　You are asking for—?

CYRANO.　　　　　　　Yes, I—
　　　[*Whispering to* CHRISTIAN.]　　Too soon!

CHRISTIAN. Now that we've shaken her, we should press on!

CYRANO [*to* ROXANE].
Yes, I—I asked—but, heavens! I should have guessed
I was presuming—

ROXANE [*a little damped*].
　　　　　　You mean you don't insist?

CYRANO. I insist—without insisting. I offended
Your modesty. We'll call the matter ended.

CHRISTIAN [*tugging at* CYRANO'S *cloak*].
Why?

CYRANO. Shut up, Christian!

ROXANE [*leaning over the balcony*]. What are you muttering?

CYRANO. Knowing I had gone too far, I was uttering
A rebuke to myself. I said 'Shut up, Christian.'—Wait!
[*A lute has begun to play off-stage.*]

[82]

Someone's coming! Sad for a man! [*The other lute plays.*]
            —And that
Is spritely for a woman!
    [ROXANE *shuts the window.* CYRANO *listens to the lutes, one playing a gay tune, the other a sad one.*]
            A strange duet,
Sad and gay together. Are the two lads drunk?
Is it a man or a woman?—Oh, I see! It's a monk.
    [*Enter a* FRIAR *who goes from house to house, a lantern in his hand, looking at the doors.*]

CYRANO [*to the* FRIAR].
What are you acting like a Diogenes for?

FRIAR. To find the house of Madame—

CHRISTIAN.   The tedious bore!

FRIAR. Madeleine Robin.

CHRISTIAN.   What does he want?

CYRANO [*pointing to another street*].   Not here!
Straight on—keep going.

FRIAR.   Thanks, you will be in my prayer.
I'll say my rosary through to the largest bead. [*He goes.*]

CYRANO. Good luck, and a blessing on your tonsured head.
           [*He goes back to* CHRISTIAN.]

CHRISTIAN. Get that kiss for me!

CYRANO.   No!

CHRISTIAN.   Sooner or later—

CYRANO.   True,
The dizzy moment will come—
    [*The window-shutters reopen.* CHRISTIAN *hides under the balcony.*]

ROXANE [*coming on to the balcony*].   Christian, is that you?
You were speaking just now of—

CYRANO.   Of a kiss. A gentle word.
I don't know why your lips find it so hard.

[83]

It's nothing, surely, to be frightened by:
Already, almost imperceptibly,
You have gone from smiles to sighing, and had no fears,
And from the sigh you have melted into tears.
There's only a little further to progress,
The hair-fine crossing between tears and kiss!

ROXANE. Oh, quiet!

CYRANO.   A kiss, what is it, after all?
The simple witness to a lover's will,
The seal that makes a promise ratified,
The longing-to-be-home half-gratified,
An unheard secret whispered to the mouth,
Coming upon the heart like the sweet south.
A claim, a gift, nature's communion-cup—

ROXANE. Climb, then, and claim this miracle!

CYRANO [*pushing* CHRISTIAN *towards the balcony*]. Climb up!

ROXANE. This longing-to-be-home!

CYRANO.   Climb!

ROXANE.   This simple witness . . .

CYRANO. Climb!

CHRISTIAN [*hesitating*].
            Now the moment's here I doubt its rightness!

ROXANE. This unheard secret . . .

CYRANO [*pushing him*].   Climb, you idiot!
    [CHRISTIAN *springs forward and climbs by way of the bench,*
    the branches, the pillars of the balcony, and leaps on to it.]

CHRISTIAN [*embraces and kisses her*].
    Ah, Roxane!

CYRANO.   The strange weight on the heart!
    There is the lovers' feast, and here I wait
    Like Lazarus in the darkness at the gate.
    But there's one crumb of comfort I can savour:
    She kisses on his mouth the words I gave her.
        [*The sound of the lutes off-stage.*]

[84]

Sad and gay together! The monk!

[*He pretends to have come running from a distance.*]

CYRANO. Hallo!

ROXANE. Who is it?

CYRANO. Is Christian there?

CHRISTIAN [*very astonished*]. Why, Cyrano!

CYRANO. I was passing.

ROXANE. Good evening, cousin!

CYRANO. Good evening, cousin!

ROXANE. I'm coming down.

[*She goes into the house.*]

[*The* FRIAR *enters.*]

CHRISTIAN [*seeing him*]. Oh *he's* back!

[*He follows* ROXANE.]

FRIAR. I'm quite certain
Madeleine Robin lives here.

CYRANO. You said: Ro-*lin.*

FRIAR. Pardon me, I said: *Bin.* B, i, n, *bin!*

[ROXANE *comes to the door, followed by* RAGUENEAU *with a lantern, and* CHRISTIAN.]

ROXANE. What is it?

FRIAR. I have to deliver to you this letter.

CHRISTIAN. Eh?

FRIAR. I'm sure it concerns a spiritual matter.
It comes from a worthy lord—

ROXANE [*to* CHRISTIAN]. De Guiche!

CHRISTIAN. Does he dare?

ROXANE. Well, he won't pester me for ever, my dear.
I love you, and so—

[*She breaks open the letter and reads quietly to herself by the light of* RAGUENEAU's *lantern.*]

'Dear Lady: the drums are beating.

[85]

My regiment is ready to leave. But I am waiting
In secret here at the monastery, in spite
Of what you said. I shall come to you tonight.
The monk who brings this letter has less guile
Than a lamb, and knows nothing of this. I cherish your
smile
At parting, and have to see you again. So pray
Be sure that you send everyone else away.
You will forgive my boldness, I hope, and deign
To receive me alone—he who will ever remain
Your very devoted etcetera . . .'
    [*To the* FRIAR.]   Father, I fear
The letter's not pleasant to me, but you shall hear:
        [*All gather round as she reads aloud.*]
'Lady, the Cardinal's wishes must be obeyed
However unwelcome to you. The decision is made.
And that, dear lady, is the reason I send
These lines for your attention by the hand
Of a saintly, discreet, and most intelligent friar,
To whom we wish you to convey our desire
That in your own house, on this very night,
He should privately perform the Holy Rite
        [*She turns over the page.*]
Of Matrimony, between you and Christian.
Overcome your repugnance. Believe that Heaven
Will reward your compliance, and rest assured
I remain your humble, etcetera . . .'

FRIAR.   Worthy lord!
As I thought, I needn't have feared bringing the letter.
I knew it must concern some spiritual matter!

ROXANE [*softly to* CHRISTIAN].
Did I read it nicely?

CHRISTIAN [*clearing his throat, warningly*].
             Hum!

ROXANE [*aloud, as in despair*]. It is horrible, this!

[86]

FRIAR [*holding his lantern to* CYRANO'*s face*].
  It refers to you?

CHRISTIAN.   To me!

FRIAR.   But—

ROXANE [*quickly*].   There's a P.S.
  'Give a hundred pistoles to the monastery.'

FRIAR. Worthy, worthy lord! [*To* ROXANE.] It has to be,
  So resign yourself.

ROXANE [*like a martyr*].
          I submit, I submit.
    [*As* RAGUENEAU *opens the door, and* CHRISTIAN *invites the*
    FRIAR *to enter, she whispers to* CYRANO.]
  Keep De Guiche at bay. You must use your wit
  To keep him out, until—

CYRANO.   Understood!—Now, Father,
  How long will it take?

FRIAR.   A quarter of an hour.

CYRANO [*shepherding them towards the house*].
  Run along, then. I'm not coming.

ROXANE [*to* CHRISTIAN].   Let us go.
          [*Exeunt all into the house.*]

CYRANO. How to detain De Guiche, I'd like to know,
  For fifteen minutes.
    [*He jumps on the bench and starts to climb to the balcony.*]
          Well, for a start, let's climb!
  I've got an idea! [*The lutes sound glumly off-stage.*]
          Aha! It's a man, this time!
    [*The tremolo on the lutes becomes sinister.*]
  No doubt about that!
    [*On the balcony, he pulls his hat over his eyes, takes off his sword,
    wraps himself in his cloak, and leans over.*]
          Right! It's not too high!
    [*He grasps a long branch of a tree by the garden wall and hangs
    on to it, ready to let himself drop.*]

Pardon me, Air, if I presume to fly!

[DE GUICHE *enters, masked, groping his way in the dark.*]

DE GUICHE. What has happened to that wretched Friar?

CYRANO. The devil! He'll recognize my voice.

[*Hanging by one hand he turns an imaginary key.*]

Cric! Crac!

I'll use the dialect of Bergerac!

DE GUICHE [*looking at the house*].

Is this it? Can't see very well. This mask's a mistake.

[*He starts to enter.* CYRANO *swings from the balcony on the branch, which drops him between the door and* DE GUICHE. *He pretends to fall heavily as though from a great height, and lies on the ground as though stunned.* DE GUICHE *leaps back.*]

DE GUICHE. Hey! What? [*When he looks up, the branch has sprung back. He sees only the sky and is amazed.*]

Where's he fallen from, for heaven's sake?

CYRANO. Out of the moon!

DE GUICHE. Out of—?

CYRANO. What's the time?

DE GUICHE. Is he out of his mind?

CYRANO. What time of day, what clime,
What day of the week? What month of the year?

DE GUICHE. But—

CYRANO. I'm half stupefied!

DE GUICHE. But, my dear sir—!

CYRANO. I fell off the moon like a thunderbolt!

DE GUICHE [*impatiently*]. Buffoon!

CYRANO [*rising, in a terrible voice*].

Off the moon, I tell you!

DE GUICHE [*recoiling*]. All right! you fell off the moon.
He's surely mad, or seriously confused.

CYRANO [*approaching him*].

Be sure that wasn't a metaphor I used!

[88]

DE GUICHE. But—

CYRANO.   A hundred years ago—or maybe a minute—
God knows how long it took me to descend—
The moon glowed in the sky, and I was in it!

DE GUICHE [*shrugging*].
Of course. Now let me pass.

CYRANO [*intercepting him*].   Where am I, friend?
Be frank! What is this region of the night
That I've crashed down on like a meteorite?

DE GUICHE. Confound it!

CYRANO.   I fell so fast I couldn't choose
A landing place, and don't know where it is.
Is this a satellite or major planet
Which took the whole weight of my backside upon it?

DE GUICHE. I tell you, sir—

CYRANO [*recoiling in mock alarm*]. Ah! Great God! Get back!
I'm in a place where faces are all black!

DE GUICHE [*putting his hand to his face*].
What?

CYRANO [*feigning terror*].
          Are you an African?

DE GUICHE [*remembering*].   This mask!

CYRANO [*pretending to be a little reassured*].
Is it Venice, then, or Genoa, may I ask?

DE GUICHE [*trying to get by*].
A lady is waiting! . . .

CYRANO [*completely reassured*].
                    I'm in Paris then!

DE GUICHE [*smiling in spite of himself*].
Humorous!

CYRANO.   You laugh?

DE GUICHE.   I do—but again
I must ask you to let me pass.

[89]

CYRANO.   So I've dropped back
   Into Paris. What a surprising stroke of luck!
      [*At ease, laughing, bowing, dusting himself down.*]
   I've come—you really must forgive me—through
   A storm of cosmic particles. A few
   Are still adhering. What a trip! My eyes
   Are sore with the astral dust that fills the skies.
   Tufts from a planet are caught up in my spurs.
              [*Picking something off his sleeve.*]
   Look here, a comet's tail has shed some hairs!

DE GUICHE [*beside himself*].
   Sir!

CYRANO [*showing him his leg*].
      I got a nip from the Great Bear.
   Avoided Neptune, but (trying to steer clear
   Of the prongs of his trident) landed up in state
   On the heavenly Scales. Now Heaven records my weight.

   [*Quickly stopping* DE GUICHE *from passing and holding him
   by a button.*]

   If you pinched my nose you'd discover, I daresay,
   That it spouted milk.

DE GUICHE.   Milk?

CYRANO.   From the Milky Way.

DE GUICHE. Oh, go to Hell!

CYRANO.   But Heaven sent me here!
              [*Folding his arms.*]
   I noticed, in passing, that Sirius seems to wear
   A nightcap when he dosses down at night.
              [*Confidentially.*]
   The Little Bear is too immature to bite.
              [*Laughing.*]
   On my way across the Lyre I snapped a string!
              [*Grandiloquently.*]
   But I mean to write a book about everything;

And the smaller stars, which I managed to catch and cage,
Will make useful asterisks on the printed page!

DE GUICHE. That's enough, I want—

CYRANO.   I know what you're afraid of:
That you won't get out of me what the moon is made of,
And whether there's any form of life or not there?

DE GUICHE. No, not at all!

CYRANO.   You're wondering how I got there?
Well, it was by a method I invented—
Brilliant, if I may say so.

DE GUICHE.   He's demented!

CYRANO. Not for me the eagle, as suggested
By Regiomontanus, or the pigeon-chested
Pigeon of Archytas—

DE GUICHE.   He is mad—
But in a highbrow way.

CYRANO.   No, I never had
Much use for other people's theories. I
Found four new ways to rape the virgin sky!*

DE GUICHE [*turning round*].
Four?

CYRANO [*volubly*]. To strip as naked as a taper,
Hang crystal phials of early-morning vapour
All round my torso, then, as the day's heat grew,
To evaporate upward with the rising dew.

DE GUICHE [*surprised, taking a step towards him*].
Well, that's one method!

CYRANO.   Also, of course, you could
Increase gale-force by making a cedar-wood
Container holding mirrors, icosahedron-wise,
Which would rarefy the air and make it rise.

DE GUICHE. That's two!

CYRANO.   Mechanically, one could devise

A metal grasshopper with steel-sprung thighs
Impelled by successive firing of saltpetre,
Which would be almost as functional, but neater.

DE GUICHE [*following him and counting on his fingers*].
Three!

CYRANO [*who has drawn* DE GUICHE *to the other side of the
Square near to a bench*].
          As you're interested, here's the last:
I sit on an iron platform. Then I cast
A giant magnet up into the air.—
Really, you know, it's a marvellous idea!—
The platform follows. I throw again, and lightly
We pursue. So on and on, indefinitely!

DE GUICHE. Four good devices! . . . Which came out of the
hat?

CYRANO. A fifth!

DE GUICHE.   Good heavens, a fifth! And what was that?

CYRANO. See if you can guess.

DE GUICHE.   I find this fascinating.

CYRANO [*making wave-noises with gestures*].
Houuh! Houuh! What's that impersonating?

DE GUICHE. Goodness, what could it be?

CYRANO.   You've got no notion?
Houuh! Houhh!

DE GUICHE.   None at all.

CYRANO.   The Atlantic Ocean! . . .
At an hour when the moon is stretching out a hand
To draw the tide, I lie down on the sand,
Having bathed in the sea—my head towards the moon,
For the hair holds water longer than the skin—
And then, and then, smooth as an angel's flight,
I soar quite effortlessly through the night:
Until I feel a sudden shock! And then—

DE GUICHE.   And then?

[92]

CYRANO. Then— [*He changes to his natural voice.*]

> The time is up. You are free again.

The wedding's over, so away you go!

DE GUICHE [*springing up*].

That voice!

[*The door of the house opens.* SERVANTS *enter carrying lighted candelabra. Light.* CYRANO *uncovers.*]

> This nose! Cyrano?

CYRANO.   Cyrano!

Here they are, united now for ever.

DE GUICHE. Who?

[*He turns and sees* ROXANE *and* CHRISTIAN, *hand in hand. The* FRIAR *follows them smiling.* RAGUENEAU *also holds a candlestick. The* DUENNA, *flurried and hastily dressed, brings up the rear.*]

DE GUICHE [*to* ROXANE].

> You? [*Recognizing* CHRISTIAN *with astonishment.*]
>
> He? [*Bowing to* ROXANE *admiringly.*]
>
> You have been supremely clever!
>
> [*To* CYRANO.]

My compliments, you master of invention:

Your story would have held a saint's attention

On his way to paradise. And such details!

No doubt the book will have enormous sales.

It will certainly make a lot of readers happy.

CYRANO. I'll see that you get a complimentary copy.

FRIAR [*indicating the lovers to* DE GUICHE].

Such a handsome pair, my son, and all your doing.

DE GUICHE. Yes. [*To* ROXANE.] Bid him farewell for the time ensuing.

ROXANE. Why?

DE GUICHE [*to* CHRISTIAN].

> The regiment is ready to leave.

Join them.

ROXANE.   To go to war?

DE GUICHE.   So I believe.

ROXANE. But the cadets don't go?

DE GUICHE.   Oh, yes, they do.
Here is the order. [*To* CHRISTIAN.] Take it to them now.

ROXANE [*in* CHRISTIAN'*s arms*].
Christian!

DE GUICHE [*to* CYRANO, *maliciously*].
            The wedding night is still far off!

CYRANO [*aside*].
By this he expects to hurt me!
        [*He turns to* CHRISTIAN *who is kissing* ROXANE.]
                              That's enough,
You must leave her, Christian.

CHRISTIAN.   To let her go,
You don't know, Cyrano, how hard it is!

CYRANO [*trying to draw him away*].   I know.
        [*The sound of drums in the distance.*]

DE GUICHE. The regiment's leaving!

ROXANE [*to* CYRANO].   I trust him to your care.
Promise his life won't be in danger—swear!

CYRANO. I'll try, but I can't promise.

ROXANE.   Promise then
That he'll be cautious!

CYRANO.   I shall do what I can.

ROXANE. See he doesn't take cold in this terrible war!

CYRANO. I—

ROXANE.   Promise he will be faithful!

CYRANO.   Oh, I'm sure—

ROXANE. And see he writes to me often, for pity's sake!

CYRANO. Now that's a promise I certainly can make!

CURTAIN

ACT FOUR

Post occupied by the company of CARBON DE CASTEL-JALOUX *at the siege of Arras.**

In the background an embankment across the whole stage. Beyond, view of plain extending to the horizon. The country covered with entrenchments. The walls of Arras and the outlines of its roofs against the sky in the distance. Tents. Arms strewn around, drums, etc. Day is breaking with a faint gleam of yellow sunrise in the east. Sentries at different points. Watch-fires. The CADETS, *wrapped in their cloaks, are sleeping.* CARBON DE CASTEL-JALOUX *and* LE BRET *keep watch. They are thin and pale.* CHRISTIAN *sleeps in the foreground, his face lighted by the fire. Silence.*

LE BRET. Disaster!

CARBON.   Yes. There's nothing to feed them on.

LE BRET. Bloody hell!

CARBON.   Curse quietly, old man,
You'll wake them. [*To the* CADETS.]
              Ssh! Go back to sleep again.
              [*To* LE BRET.]
When they sleep, they dine.

LE BRET.   The unlucky ones
Who can't sleep feel the hunger in their bones!
       [*Gun-fire is heard in the distance.*]

CARBON. Confound that firing! They're going to wake my
    boys!
       [*To* CADETS *who lift their heads.*]
Go to sleep!
      [*They lie down again. Renewed firing, nearer.*]

A CADET [*stirring*]. The devil! . . . What's the noise?

CARBON. It's nothing. It's only Cyrano coming back.
  [*The wakers put down their heads again.*]

A SENTINEL [*off-stage*].
  Halt! Who goes there?

THE VOICE OF CYRANO.   De Bergerac!

ANOTHER SENTINEL [*on the parapet*].
  Halt! Who goes there?

CYRANO [*appearing on the ridge*]. De Bergerac,
  You idiot!
      [*He comes down.* LE BRET *goes anxiously to him.*]

LE BRET.   Thank God you're safely back!

CYRANO [*signing not to wake the others*].
  Quiet!

LE BRET. Are you wounded?

CYRANO.   Me? Wounded? How?
  It's become like second nature with them now
  To miss me!

LE BRET.   Still, it's a damned foolish way
  To risk your life at sunrise every day,
  For the sake of a letter!

CYRANO.   I promised without fail
  He'd often write.—He's sleeping. He looks pale.
  If Roxane knew he was starving to death . . . But ever
  Handsome!

LE BRET.   Go and get some sleep.

CYRANO.   You never
  Stop growling, Le Bret!—I've taken pains
  To discover a passage through the Spanish lines
  Where they're always drunk.

LE BRET.   One day, perhaps, you might
  Bring us back some food.

CYRANO.   I have to travel light.
  But something unexpected will happen today.

[96]

We French are either going to eat or die,
Judging by what I've seen.

LE BRET.   What was it?

CYRANO.   No,
I'm not sure. You'll see.

CARBON.   Pretty ironical, though,
The besieging army being the one that starves!

LE BRET. The situation is like a web of nerves:
We lay siege to Arras, get trapped, and the Prince
Of Spain besieges us.

CYRANO.   Someone with sense
Should come and besiege *him*.

LE BRET.   It isn't a joke.

CYRANO. Oh! Oh!

LE BRET.   To think that every day you took
Your life in your hands for a letter. The risk to run!
Where are you going?

CYRANO.   To write another one.
                    [*He disappears into the tent.*]
[*The day is breaking. Cannon-fire is heard in the distance, followed by the sound of drums far away to the left. Other drums are
heard much nearer. Sounds of stirring in the camp. Voices of
officers in the distance.*]

CARBON [*with a sigh*]. Reveille, alas!
                    [*The* CADETS *begin to stir and stretch.*]
                                    I know what their cry will be
As soon as they're awake.

A CADET [*sitting up*].   My God! I'm hungry!

ANOTHER. I shan't last long!

CARBON.   Get up!

3RD CADET.   I can't move a step!

4TH CADET. Or raise a hand!

[97]

1ST CADET [*looking at himself in some armour*].

                 My tongue looks like old crêpe!

ANOTHER. I'll swap my coronet for a lick of cheese!

ANOTHER. My belly says 'Skulk in your tent, son, like Achilles!'

ANOTHER. Bread, bread, bread!

CARBON [*calling quietly at* CYRANO's *tent*].

                 Cyrano!

OTHER CADETS.   We're going to die!

CARBON [*still quietly, to* CYRANO].
Come outside! You're better at this than I,
Come and cheer them up!

2ND CADET [*rushing up to the* 1ST CADET].

               What are you chewing, please?

1ST CADET. A bit of gun-wadding fried in axle-grease,
There's not much grouse-shooting hereabout!

ANOTHER [*entering*].
I've been out shooting!

ANOTHER [*following him*]. I went fishing!

CADETS [*mobbing them*].   What
Luck did you have?—A ptarmigan?—A trout?—
Let's have a look!

THE ANGLER.   A gudgeon!

THE HUNTER.   A cock sparrow!

ALL [*exasperated*].
That's the last straw! Let's mutiny!

CARBON.   Cyrano!
Come and help!

            [*Daylight has come.*]

  [CYRANO *comes out of his tent, quite calm, a pen behind his ear,
a book in his hand.*]

CYRANO.   Hey! What is it?

          [*Silence. To the* 1ST CADET.]

               Son,

Why are you dragging your feet?

THE CADET.   My belly's gone
Down into my boots.

CYRANO.   And so has mine!

THE CADET. Uncomfortable, isn't it?

CYRANO.   A gain
Of height, if you stand upon it.

2ND CADET.   Mine is hollow!

CYRANO. Use it as a drum to sound the advance, dear fellow.

3RD CADET. There's a ringing in my ears.

CYRANO.   Are you trying to tell
Me that your ears are wanting food as well?

1ST CADET [*shrugging*].
Always the clever phrase!

CYRANO.   Why, yes, the phrase,
The point driven home!—The way I would choose to die
Would be at evening under a glowing sky,
Saying a good thing in a good cause!
Killed by the only weapon I respect
By a foe the gods thought fitting to elect—
On a battlefield, not a fevered bed—the sword
Piercing my heart while I spoke the lunging word!

CADETS. We're hungry, though!

CYRANO.   Can't any of you boys
Think of anything but eating?—Bertrandou,
Come over here, and bring your fife with you;
You've been a shepherd; play to this greedy crew
Some of the old tunes of Gascony.
Give us their strange, obsessive, rhythmic cry,
Each note like a young sister in the memory;
All the voices we love are in these airs,
Their slowness is the rising smoke of fires
Over the roofs; the music seems to come
Speaking the country dialect of our home.

[*The old man starts to play a tune of Languedoc.*]
Listen—under his fingers the shrill note
Of the fife has changed into the woodland flute!
It's no longer the call of war that comes from his lips
But shepherds singing in their scarlet caps,
The river at evening flowing gently by.
Listen, you Gascons: it is Gascony.
 [*The* CADETS *sit with bowed heads, dreaming; some brush away
 a tear.*]

CARBON [*to* CYRANO *in a whisper*].
You're making them weep.

CYRANO.   They're homesick. It's a state
Better than hunger! I'm glad to see the hurt
Leaving their stomachs to invade the heart.

CARBON. But you'll weaken their will to fight.

CYRANO.   Not I. There's no harm.
The courage in them will wake at the first alarm.
It only needs—
 [*He signals to the drummer who starts to beat his drum.*]

THE CADETS [*hurrying to take up arms*].
            Hey! What is it, that drum?

CYRANO. You see, it's enough: a drum-roll. They all fly to
Arms: the dreams of home are said goodbye to.
What the fife made drowsy wakes again with the drum.

A CADET [*looking off-stage*].
Here's Monsieur de Guiche!
            [*The* CADETS *murmur among themselves.*]

CYRANO [*smiling*].   A flattering welcome!

A CADET. We're sick to death of him!

ANOTHER.   With his lace collar
Spreading its peacock's tail over his armour!

1ST CADET. Like balancing a lamb on top of a lion!

2ND CADET. Always the courtier!

CARBON.   None the less, a scion
  Of Gascony!

1ST CADET.   But spurious! Beware!
  A Gascon should be as mad as a March hare:
  A rational Gascon is positively dangerous.

LE BRET. He looks pale!

ANOTHER.   He's hungry, like the rest of us,
  But his breast-plate's got so many jewels on
  The cramp in his stomach glitters in the sun!

CYRANO [quickly].
  We don't want to look as though we had the gripes!
  Get out the cards and dice, and light your pipes! . . .
      [They all quickly use the drums as card-tables, start throwing
      dice, their cloaks spread on the ground, and light their long clay
      pipes.
      CYRANO walks up and down reading a book. DE GUICHE
      enters. Everybody seems to be absorbed and content. DE GUICHE
      goes up to CARBON.]

DE GUICHE [to CARBON].
  Good-morning!—So these are the young bears
  With the sore heads?—Gentlemen, it appears
  That I'm unpopular with you country squires
  And mountain-bred nobility, the peers
  Of Perigord. You not only show disdain
  For your Colonel, but are calling him a vain,
  Intriguing courtier—and never cease
  Fuming amongst yourselves that I wear lace
  Above my armour: as though one couldn't show
  A Gascon style without looking a scarecrow!
          [Silence. They go on smoking and playing.]
  Do you want to make me order your Captain here
  To punish you? No.

CARBON.   Nor am I aware
  That you have the right. This is my company;

I bear the cost. The orders I obey
Come from the High Command.

DE GUICHE.   What? That's enough!
[*Addressing the* CADETS.]
I can afford to shrug your insolence off.
It's well known how I conduct myself in war.
Yesterday, many witnessed how I bore
Down on the Count de Bucquoi and scattered his men.
Hurling my troop like an avalanche of stone
I charged three times!

CYRANO [*without looking up from his book*].
                              Mention your white scarf!

DE GUICHE [*surprised and pleased*].
You heard about that? But no doubt only half
The story. As I was bringing my horse about
To charge for the third time, I found myself caught
In an eddy of fleeing men who swept me near
The enemy line. I could see I was in danger
Of being shot or taken prisoner.
But luckily I had the presence of mind
To untie the scarf and throw it to the ground;
So then, being inconspicuous, I could go
Back, and rally my men for the crushing blow!
—What do you say to that?
[*The* CADETS *pretend not to be listening, but the cards and dice-boxes remain suspended. They wait.*]

CYRANO.   Henry of Navarre,
However outnumbered, would have had more care
Of his white plume.
[*Silent delight. The cards fall, the dice rattle.*]

DE GUICHE.   However, the plan did work!
[*Again the attentive pause from the games-players.*]

CYRANO. No doubt it did. But an officer doesn't shirk
The honour of being a target.

[*Cards and dice fall again, and the* CADETS *smoke with obvious satisfaction.*]

CYRANO.   If I'd been there
When the scarf was dropped—the courage we have, mon-
  sieur,
Is of different kinds—I should have picked it up
And worn it.

DE GUICHE.   Gascon boasting always on tap!

CYRANO. Boasting! Lend it to me. I'll guarantee
When we make the first assault tonight you'll see
I'm wearing it.

DE GUICHE.   Another Gascon boast!
You know already that the scarf is lost,
And since then the place has been under constant fire—
No one could go and get it!

CYRANO [*drawing it from his pocket*].
                          I have it here.
[*Silence. The* CADETS *stifle their laughter in the cards and dice-boxes.* DE GUICHE *turns and looks at them; they immediately look grave and return to their games. One of them casually whistles the tune just played on the fife.*]

DE GUICHE [*taking the scarf*].
Thank you. I can make use of it now
To signal with. I was hesitating how
The message should be given.
[*He climbs on to the parapet, and waves the scarf above his head several times.*]

THE CADETS.   What is he up to? Eh?

THE SENTRY [*on the parapet*].
There's a man over there running away!

DE GUICHE [*coming down*].
A Spanish spy. I've got him in our pay.
The information he takes to the enemy
Is what I give to him: so, ingeniously,
We have control over their strategy.

[103]

CYRANO. A treacherous scoundrel!

DE GUICHE [*nonchalantly tying on the scarf*].

                          But a useful one.
—There's something you don't know. The Marshal has gone
In secret to our supply-base at Dourlens
In a desperate attempt to reprovision.
He has taken, for safe cover, so many with him
If the Spaniards attack they'll find it child's play.
We've no more than half an army to keep them at bay.

CARBON. But they don't know this.

DE GUICHE.   As a matter of fact, they do.
They're going to attack.

CARBON.   Ah!

DE GUICHE.   My spy came through
To warn me of it. He asked me to decide
Where the attack should come, and I replied:
'Watch the whole line. My choice will be at some
Point which I shall give my signal from.'

CARBON [*to the* CADETS].
Well, that's it, gentlemen!
    [ALL *get up, and start buckling on swords and breastplates.*]

DE GUICHE.   The attack will come
In an hour or so.

1ST CADET.   Oh well! No hurry, then.
        [*They all sit down and go on with their games.*]

DE GUICHE [*to* CARBON].
The Marshal will be back, but we need to gain
Time until he can get here.

CARBON.   If we can.

DE GUICHE. You will please lay down your lives to the last man.

CYRANO. And so you take your revenge?

DE GUICHE.   No one pretends
   That if I had loved you better, you and your friends,
   There might not have been a different choice. And yet
   You are all unrivalled in courage, don't forget,
   So I serve the King by serving my own mood.

CYRANO [*saluting*].
   Allow me, sir, to express our gratitude.

DE GUICHE [*saluting*].
   I know your pleasure is to fight one man
   Against a hundred, and now once more you can!
                  [*He goes upstage with* CARBON.]

CYRANO [*to the* CADETS].
   Well, gentlemen, the arms of Gascony,
   With its six chevrons of azure and gold, will carry
   Now what was lacking in this brotherhood;
   A seventh chevron, the colour of our blood.
      [DE GUICHE *converses quietly with* CARBON DE CASTEL-
      JALOUX *upstage. Commands are given. Preparations for resisting
      the attack.* CYRANO *goes to* CHRISTIAN *who stands motionless
      with folded arms.*]

CYRANO [*putting a hand on his shoulder*].
   Christian?

CHRISTIAN [*shaking his head*].
                  Roxane!

CYRANO.   I know.

CHRISTIAN.   I want you to say
   Everything that's in my heart in a way
   She will never forget, a last letter.

CYRANO.   I thought it
   Might be needed today.
                  [*He takes a letter from his coat.*]
                                   Here, I've brought it.

CHRISTIAN. Show me!

CYRANO.   You want to read it?

[105]

CHRISTIAN [*taking the letter*].   Of course, why not?
     [*He opens it, starts reading and suddenly looks up.*]
   Good lord!

CYRANO.   What?

CHRISTIAN.   This smudge of ink . . .

CYRANO [*taking back the letter*].   Oh, that.

CHRISTIAN. It's a tear stain!

CYRANO.   Yes; a poet has to feel
   That whatever he is imagining is real.
   Writing this letter for you while you slept
   The words became such a part of me—

CHRISTIAN.   You wept?

CYRANO. Because—though death itself isn't terrible—
   Yet—never to see her again—that's unbearable!
   I may never—
                    [CHRISTIAN *looks at him.*]
                    —we may never . . .
                              [*quickly*] —you may never . . .

CHRISTIAN [*snatching the note*].
   Give me the letter!
          [*The noise of excitement in the camp in the distance.*]

THE VOICE OF A SENTRY. Halt! Who goes there?
          [*A shot or two. Voices shouting. Carriage bells.*]

CARBON. What is it?

SENTRY [*on the parapet*]. A carriage!
                    [*A rush to look.*]

CRIES.   In the camp? It's driving through—
   As though from the Spanish lines! What do we do?
   Fire on it! No! The coachman is shouting something!
   He said 'In the King's service!'
          [*Everybody is on the parapet, staring off-stage. The carriage bells
          get nearer.*]

DE GUICHE.   What? From the King!
          [*They all come down and form up in line.*]

[106]

CARBON. Hats off!

DE GUICHE [*into the wings*].

Clear the way! Can't you see the carriage is turning?
[*The carriage comes on at a smart pace, covered in mud and dust.
Two lackeys up behind. The curtains are closed. It stops short.*]
Sound the drums! Let down the step!
[*Roll of drums. All the* CADETS *uncovered.*]

ROXANE [*jumping from the carriage*].   Good morning!
[*At the sound of a woman's voice, every head is raised. Sensation.*]

DE GUICHE. In the King's service? You?

ROXANE.   King love, my friend,
The only one.

CYRANO.   Great God!

CHRISTIAN.   Why are you here,
Roxane?

ROXANE.   It's gone on too long, this wretched war.

CHRISTIAN. But why?—

ROXANE.   I shall tell you.

CYRANO [*who has not turned to look at her*].

                                      Dare I see her again?

DE GUICHE. You can't stay here!

ROXANE [*gaily*].   I can, of course I can!
May I have a drum to sit on?
                      [*A* CADET *brings one.*]
                              You're a willing soul:
Thank you. [*She laughs.*]
              My carriage was fired at! [*Proudly.*] By a patrol!
—It's rather like the pumpkin, wouldn't you say,
Which turned into a coach, and the footmen—they
Used to be mice. [*Throwing a kiss to* CHRISTIAN.]
                      Good morning!—You don't look gay,
Any of you!—It seemed a long, long way
To Arras. [*Noticing* CYRANO.]
                Cousin, how lovely!

[107]

CYRANO.   You alarm me!
  How on earth—

ROXANE.   —did I manage to find the army?
  My friend, it was only too easy. I took the road
  Which led through devastation. O my God,
  It has to be seen to be believed. Gentlemen,
  If this is the King's service, I prefer my own!

CYRANO. Madness! There's no way to get here whatever!

ROXANE. Through the Spanish lines.

1ST CADET.   My God! Women are clever!

DE GUICHE. But how?

LE BRET.   A desperately difficult way to try!

ROXANE. No, not really. I simply passed them by
  At a smart trot. Whenever I caught the eye
  Of a fierce hidalgo, I gave him my nicest smile,
  And those gentlemen being (with due respect to all
  You Frenchmen) the most gallant on this earth,
  They let me pass.

CARBON.   I know your smile is worth
  Any number of passports. Even so
  They must sometimes have asked you where you meant to
    go.

ROXANE. Frequently. And I told them: 'I'm on the way
  To see my lover.' At which, immediately
  Even the fiercest Spaniard solemnly
  Shut the carriage door, waving away
  The muskets pointing at me, with a regal
  Gesture and the stern grace of an eagle,
  The plume on his hat floating in the breeze,
  And bowed and said: 'Pass, señorita, please!'

CHRISTIAN. But, Roxane—

ROXANE.   I said 'My lover.' Please forgive me.
  If I'd said 'My husband', Christian, believe me
  They wouldn't have let me pass!

CHRISTIAN. No, but—

ROXANE. What, then?

DE GUICHE. You must leave here.

ROXANE. I?

CYRANO. And leave at once, Roxane.

LE BRET. As soon as you can!

CHRISTIAN. Yes!

ROXANE. But, why?

CHRISTIAN [*embarrassed*]. Because . . .

CYRANO [*also embarrassed*].
In three quarters of an hour—

DE GUICHE. More or less . . .

CARBON. It would be best—

LE BRET. If you—

ROXANE. You're going to fight!
I shall stay.

ALL. No!

ROXANE. He's my husband! [*She throws herself
in* CHRISTIAN's *arms.*] It's my right
To die with him!

DE GUICHE [*despairing*].
This particular post
Is a terrible one.

ROXANE [*turning*]. Terrible?

CYRANO. The worst.
And the proof of it is that he put us here!

ROXANE [*to* DE GUICHE].
You want to make me a widow?

DE GUICHE. No, I swear!—

ROXANE. Today I'm feeling reckless! I'm not willing
To go away. Moreover, I find it thrilling.

CYRANO. What's this? Our lady of wit a heroine?

ROXANE. Monsieur de Bergerac, I am your cousin.

A CADET. We'll defend you to the death!

ROXANE. I know you will,
My friends!

ANOTHER [*ecstatic*]. The whole camp has the sweet smell
Of a summer garden!

ROXANE. And by a happy chance
The hat I'm wearing suits the circumstance
Of a battle nicely! [*Looking at* DE GUICHE.]
Perhaps the time has come
For the Count to be discreet and make for home.
The fighting may start soon.

DE GUICHE. This can't be borne!
I shall go and inspect the guns. When I return
You will have had the time to change your mind.

ROXANE. Never!

[DE GUICHE *goes*.]

CHRISTIAN [*entreating*].
Roxane!

ROXANE. No!

1ST CADET [*to the others*]. She means to stay here!

ALL [*rushing about tidying themselves up*]. Find
A comb! Soap! My uniform is torn!
A needle! Your mirror! My cuffs are badly worn!
Where are some curling tongs for my moustache?
Bring me to a razor! When did you last wash?

ROXANE [*to* CYRANO *who still implores her*].
No! Nothing will make me leave this place!
[CARBON, *who, like the others, has been dusting himself down,
arranging his belt and cuffs, comes to* ROXANE.]

CARBON. Perhaps I should introduce you, in that case,
To some of these young gentlemen of France

Who will have the honour of dying in your presence.
[ROXANE *bows, and waits, leaning on* CHRISTIAN'*s arm.*
CARBON *makes the introductions.*]
Baron de Peyrescous de Colignac!

THE CADET [*saluting*].   Madame.

CARBON. Baron de Casterac de Cahuzac. —Vidame
De Malgouyre Estressac Lesbas d'Escarabiot.—
Chevalier d'Antignac-Juzet.—Baron Hillot
De Blagnac-Salechan de Castel-Crabioules . . .

ROXANE. How many names to each of you, as a rule?

BARON HILLOT. Dozens!

CARBON [*to* ROXANE].   Drop your handkerchief.

ROXANE [*letting it fall*].   Why, what for?
[*The whole company start forward to pick it up.*]

CARBON [*quickly retrieving it*].
Our company is without a flag! But here
Is the finest in the camp!

ROXANE.   It's rather small.

CARBON [*tying it to his lance*]. But made of lace!

A CADET [*to the others*].   I shouldn't mind death at all
After seeing this vision, if only I had
Something inside me equivalent to food!

CARBON [*overhearing him, indignantly*].
You should be ashamed of yourself, thinking about
Food when a lovely woman—

ROXANE.   There's no doubt
The fresh air here creates an appetite;
I'm famished. Partridge pie and cherry tart
And some good wine, that's my bill of fare!
—Would someone fetch it for me, please?

A CADET.   From where,
For God's sake?

ROXANE.   Out of my carriage.

[111]

ALL.   What?

ROXANE. Someone must carve and serve it—I forgot
    To present my coachman to you. You will know
    A good man when you see him.

THE CADETS [*hurrying to the carriage*].
                            It's Ragueneau!

ROXANE [*looking after them*].
    Poor fellows!

CYRANO [*kissing her hand*].
             Good angel!

RAGUENEAU [*standing on the box like a mountebank at a fair*].
                        Gentlemen . . . !

THE CADETS.   Bravo!
    Bravo! Speech!

RAGUENEAU.   The Spaniards weren't aware
    That when they let past the divinely fair
    They also let by the divine repast!
                  [*Applause.*]

CYRANO [*quietly to* CHRISTIAN].
    Christian, listen!

RAGUENEAU.   Preoccupied to the last
    With gallantry, they missed the galantine!
    [*Applause. The galantine passes from hand to hand.*]

CYRANO [*to* CHRISTIAN].
    I must have a word!

RAGUENEAU.   While motioning Venus on,
    Dazzled they overlooked the venison!
        [*Enthusiasm. Hands grasp the leg of venison.*]

CYRANO to [CHRISTIAN]
    I want to talk to you!

ROXANE [*to the* CADETS *who have come back, their arms full of
    food.*]
                Put it there on the ground.

[*She begins to arrange things on the grass, helped by two imperturbable lackeys who rode behind on the carriage.*]

[*to* CHRISTIAN, *whom* CYRANO *is endeavouring to lead aside*].
Make yourself useful!

[CHRISTIAN *goes to help.* CYRANO *looks worried.*]

RAGUENEAU.   Truffled peacock!

1ST CADET [*radiant, and coming from the carriage with a large ham*].
                                        I'm bound
To say, heaven knows we're not going to face a sudden
Death without a proper blow-out—

                [*Correcting himself on seeing* ROXANE.]
                                        Pardon!

Banquet!

RAGUENEAU [*throwing down cushions from the carriage*].
                The cushions are stuffed with ortolons!

[*Hubbub. They rip open the cushions. Laughter. Merriment.*]

3RD CADET. I say!!

RAGUENEAU [*throwing down bottles of wine*].
                                Flasks of ruby! There's romance!

Flasks of topaz!

ROXANE [*throwing a folded cloth at* CYRANO].
                        There, unfold that, please!

And quickly!

RAGUENEAU [*waving a lamp*].
                The carriage-lamps—in each of these
Is a miniature larder!

CYRANO [*to* CHRISTIAN, *while they unfold the tablecloth together*].
                                I've got to talk to you
Before you talk to her!

RAGUENEAU [*waxing more and more lyrical*].
                                A whip, it's true,
But the handle a length of sausage!

ROXANE [*pouring wine and passing food*]. Since it's we
Who are put in the path of death, we can agree

[113]

To disregard the rest of the army. See!
Everything for the Gascons!—And if de Guiche
Comes back we leave him nothing within reach!
    [*Going from one to the other.*]

You've plenty of time.—Don't eat so quickly—Drink
A little—What are you crying for?

IST CADET.   I think
It's all a dream!

ROXANE.   Then dream it!—Red or white?
Some bread for Monsieur de Carbon!—Pass your plate!
You need a knife!—Have a biscuit!—Are you wanting
More? You shall have it!
    [CYRANO *is following her, his arms piled with plates, helping
    to serve.*]

CYRANO [*to himself*].   She is enchanting!

ROXANE [*going to* CHRISTIAN].
What for you?

CHRISTIAN.   Nothing.

ROXANE.   If only a biscuit
And a sip of Muscatel?

CHRISTIAN [*trying to detain her*].
                  What made you risk it,
Coming here?

ROXANE.   When I've finished waiting on
These unhappy boys. I promise to tell you soon!
    [LE BRET *has gone up to the rampart to pass a loaf on the end
    of a lance to the* SENTRY.]

LE BRET. De Guiche!

CYRANO.   Quick, hide everything away!
Jump to it! Don't leave anything on display!
And try to look miserable.
[*To* RAGUENEAU.]   Up you get,
Ragueneau, on to your box!—Is that the lot?

[*In an instant everything has been pushed into the tents or hidden under cloaks and coats.* DE GUICHE *enters hurriedly, then stops, sniffing the air. Silence.*]

DE GUICHE. That's a good smell.

A CADET [*casually singing*].   Tol-de-riddle-o!

DE GUICHE [*stopping and looking at him*].   What
Is the matter with you? You're looking very red.

THE CADET. I? Nothing. A rush of blood to the head
At the thought of battle.

ANOTHER.   Pompetty pom!

DE GUICHE [*turning round*].   What's wrong?

THE CADET [*slightly drunk*].
Wrong, sir? Nothing. I was singing a little song.

DE GUICHE. You're all in great spirits!

THE CADET.   There's a fight in view!

DE GUICHE [*calling* CARBON *to him to give him an order*].
Captain, I—Damn it! You're looking cheerful, too!

CARBON [*crimson in the face, and hiding a bottle behind him*].
Oh, am I?

DE GUICHE.   There was an extra cannon. I had it
Brought up here. Your men are going to need it.

A CADET [*swaying*].
How very kind!

ANOTHER.   Most thoughtful!

DE GUICHE.   Have they all
Gone mad? [*Drily.*] Remember a cannon will recoil,
So be careful.

1ST CADET.   Rubbish!

DE GUICHE [*furiously*].   Look here—!

THE CADET.   A Gascon gun
Never recoils!

DE GUICHE [*shaking him by the shoulder*].
I believe you're drunk! What on?

[115]

THE CADET [*superbly*].
  The smell of powder!

DE GUICHE [*shrugging and going to* ROXANE].
                Now, madam, perhaps you'll deign
  To tell me your decision?

ROXANE.   I remain.

DE GUICHE. I beg you to leave!

ROXANE.   I refuse.

DE GUICHE.   Well, if that's so,
  Hand me a musket!

CARBON.   Why?

DE GUICHE.   I stay here, too.

CYRANO. At last, here's proper courage!

IST CADET.   And a true
  Gascon, in spite of the lace!

ROXANE.   Why will you stay?

DE GUICHE. I won't desert a lady in peril.

2ND CADET [*to the* IST].   I say!
  Don't you think he deserves something to eat?
    [*All the remainder of the feast appears as by magic.*]

DE GUICHE [*his eyes shining*].
  Food!

3RD CADET. Appearing from under every coat!

DE GUICHE [*recovering self-control, haughtily*].
  And do you really suppose I'm going to eat
  Your leavings?

CYRANO [*saluting*]. You're progressing!

DE GUICHE [*fiercely, slipping into dialect*]. I'd rather fight
  On an empty stom-ach!*

IST CADET [*exulting*].   Stom-ach! Listen, he's got
  A Gascony accent!

DE GUICHE [*laughing*]. I?

[116]

THE CADET.   He's one of our lot!
   [*They start to dance.*]
   [CARBON DE CASTEL-JALOUX, *who had disappeared behind
   the parapet, reappears on the ridge.*]

CARBON. The pikemen are drawn up, ready to hold the line.
   [*He points to a line of pikes which show above the parapet.*]

DE GUICHE [*bowing to* ROXANE].
   Will you take my arm, and come and review these men?
   [*She takes it, they go up on to the parapet. Everyone else uncovers
   and follows.*]

CHRISTIAN [*hurrying to* CYRANO].
   Now's your chance!
   [*As* ROXANE *appears on the parapet, the lances disappear,
   lowered in salute, and a shout goes up. She bows.*]

PIKEMEN [*off-stage*].   Hurrah!

CHRISTIAN.   What's on your mind?

CYRANO. Just in case Roxane—

CHRISTIAN.   Well?

CYRANO.   You may find
   She mentions your letters—

CHRISTIAN.   Quite likely, I suppose!

CYRANO. Well, don't be a fool and show any surprise.

CHRISTIAN. What about?

CYRANO.   I have to explain—it's all
   Quite simple. It didn't occur to me until
   I saw her this morning. You have written, you see—

CHRISTIAN. Well, come on!

CYRANO.   You've written more frequently
   Than you thought you had.

CHRISTIAN.   Really?

CYRANO.   Yes, indeed.
   I'd taken it on myself, as we agreed,

[117]

To express your thoughts in a way she would find exciting.
And I've written sometimes without saying I was writing.

CHRISTIAN. Have you?

CYRANO.   It's all quite simple!

CHRISTIAN.   Was it so?
Since we've been cut off, how did you get them through?

CYRANO. Oh! I could slip through the lines before daybreak.

CHRISTIAN. You call that simple! And how many times a
    week
Have I been writing to her? Two?—Three?
Four times?

CYRANO.   More.

CHRISTIAN.   Every day?

CYRANO.   Yes, every day.
Twice.

CHRISTIAN [violently].
                And you got so carried away you were
Risking death daily—

CYRANO [seeing ROXANE returning].
                            Ssh! Not in front of her!
    [He hurries into his tent.]
    [In the distance CADETS coming and going. CARBON and DE
    GUICHE give orders.]

ROXANE [running to CHRISTIAN].
And now, Christian!

CHRISTIAN [taking her hands].
                            And now perhaps you'll tell
What made you make this journey into hell?

ROXANE. Your letters!

CHRISTIAN.   What?

ROXANE.   Lay the blame at your own door
That I dared to brave the dangers of the war.
Your letters made me light-headed! Do you know

[118]

How many you have written, this month or so?
And each one more wonderful!

CHRISTIAN.   And for a few
Love-letters—

ROXANE.   Be quiet! How can you know?
Ever since that summer evening when
A voice I scarcely recognized began
To show how deep your nature could be measured,
I've worshipped you. And now in all these treasured
Letters, I've heard that evening voice still clear,
Still pleading. Blame yourself that I am here.
The wise Penelope would never have stayed
Weaving at home if her Ulysses had
Written as you have. To reach his side,
As impetuous as Helen, she would have rolled
The balls of wool half way across the world!

CHRISTIAN. But—

ROXANE.   I have read them, and re-read them, till
   my head
Swam with their incantation. In every word
That blazed from every page of them, I'd hear
The depth and sincerity . . .

CHRISTIAN.   Deep and sincere?
They seemed like that, Roxane?

ROXANE.   True things they taught me.

CHRISTIAN. And is that why you came here?

ROXANE.   They have brought me
To ask your forgiveness (and what better hour
To ask forgiveness than when death is near?)
For all the shallowness that I have shown
By first loving your beauty and that alone.

CHRISTIAN [*horrified*].
Oh, Roxane!

ROXANE.   And then, more worthily—

[119]

As a young bird hops before it learns to fly—
Your body and soul were inseparate, and I knew
I loved them both, equally.

CHRISTIAN.   And now?

ROXANE. Ah, now! At last reality prevails.
I love your inner self above all else.

CHRISTIAN [*drawing back*].
Oh, Roxane!

ROXANE.   Be happy, that being so.
To be loved only for the outward show
Would be torment to a heart as great as yours;
But what you look like your rich mind outsoars,
And the beauty, which at first meant most to me,
Now that I see clearly, I no longer see!

CHRISTIAN. Oh!

ROXANE.   You still doubt how victorious you are?

CHRISTIAN. Roxane!

ROXANE.   I understand: you hardly dare
Believe such love?

CHRISTIAN.   Nor want such love, I say!
I simply want to be loved—

ROXANE.   In the usual way
That women have always loved you up to now?
This is a better love than you ever knew!

CHRISTIAN. No! It was best before!

ROXANE.   You don't understand!
I out-love now all the loving in the land!
Don't you see? Your real identity is what I adore.
If you were less handsome—

CHRISTIAN.   Don't!

ROXANE.   I'd love you more!
If all your beauty vanished in the night—

CHRISTIAN. Don't say it!

[120]

ROXANE.   I will!

CHRISTIAN.   And I became a sight?

ROXANE. Yes, then for certain!

CHRISTIAN.   God!

ROXANE.   Are you happy now?

CHRISTIAN [*in a choked voice*]. Yes . . .

ROXANE.   What is it?

CHRISTIAN.   Nothing. A word or two:
I won't be long.

ROXANE.   But—

CHRISTIAN [*gently directing her*].
                              Our happiness deprives
All these poor chaps, who soon may lose their lives,
Of having the comfort of your smile—so go!

ROXANE [*touched*].
    Dear Christian!
    [*She goes up to the* CADETS *who respectfully crowd round her,
    while* CHRISTIAN *calls outside* CYRANO'S *tent.*]

CHRISTIAN.   Cyrano?

CYRANO [*coming out, armed for battle*].
                              What's wrong with you?

CHRISTIAN. She doesn't love me any longer?

CYRANO.   No?

CHRISTIAN. It's you, it's you she loves!

CYRANO.   Don't be a fool!

CHRISTIAN. Cyrano, she only loves my soul!

CYRANO. No!

CHRISTIAN.   Yes! Which means that she loves *you*—
And you love her as well.

CYRANO.   You think I do?

CHRISTIAN. Yes.

CYRANO.   Well, it's true.

CHRISTIAN. To madness.

CYRANO. More than that.

CHRISTIAN. Tell her so!

CYRANO. No!

CHRISTIAN. Why not?

CYRANO. Do you forget?
  Look at my face.

CHRISTIAN. She would love me still, she says,
  If I were ugly!

CYRANO. She really said that?

CHRISTIAN. Yes!

CYRANO. I bless her for it! But don't believe a word
  Of anything so palpably absurd.
  (Dear God, it's pleasing, though.) Go back, you brute—
  Don't lose your looks, I'd have to follow suit!

CHRISTIAN. Well, let's find out!

CYRANO. No, no!

CHRISTIAN. And let her choose.
  You must tell her everything!

CYRANO. No, I refuse
  To be racked!

CHRISTIAN. Can I kill your happiness because
  Of the face I happen to have? It would be unjust!

CYRANO. Do you think I'd stamp your happiness in the dust
  Because, by a fluke of nature, I can dress
  In words what you may feel but can't express?

CHRISTIAN. Tell her everything!

CYRANO. Get behind me, devil!

CHRISTIAN. I'm sick of being my own most dangerous rival!

CYRANO. Christian!

CHRISTIAN. Our marriage—secret, without witnesses—
  Can be dissolved—if we survive, that is.

[122]

CYRANO. You're determined.

CHRISTIAN. Yes, determined: because I will
Be loved for what I am, or not at all!
—I'll go and inspect the forward post while you
Have it out with her. I shall come back to know
Which of us she prefers.

CYRANO. It will be you!

CHRISTIAN. Perhaps—I hope so! [*He calls.*] Roxane!

CYRANO. No, Christian, no!

ROXANE [*coming up quickly*].
What is it?

CHRISTIAN. Cyrano has something important to say.
[ROXANE *hastens to* CYRANO. CHRISTIAN *goes.*]

ROXANE. Something important?

CYRANO [*distracted*]. He has gone away!
[*To* ROXANE.]
It's nothing! You know what he's like, Roxane, and how
He attaches importance to nothing.

ROXANE. Even now
He doubts what I told him? I could see he did.

CYRANO [*taking her hand*].
But was it really true, Roxane, what you said?

ROXANE. Yes, that I'd love him even— [*She hesitates.*]

CYRANO [*smiling sadly*]. Do you find it
Awkward to say to my face?

ROXANE. But—

CYRANO. I don't mind it—
Even ugly?

ROXANE. Even ugly!
[*The sound of gunfire.*]
—Did you hear a shot?

CYRANO. Hideous?

ROXANE. Hideous!

[123]

CYRANO. Disfigured?

ROXANE. Disfigured!

CYRANO. But not
Grotesque?

ROXANE. Nothing could make him grotesque to me!

CYRANO. You would still love him?

ROXANE. More abundantly!

CYRANO [losing his head, aside].
Oh God! Can I be happy? It may be true.
[To ROXANE.]
I . . . Roxane . . . listen! . . .

LE BRET [running on, then quietly]. Cyrano!

CYRANO [turning from ROXANE]. Eh?
[LE BRET whispers into CYRANO's ear.]

CYRANO [letting go ROXANE's hand with a cry].
Ah!

ROXANE. What's wrong?

CYRANO [to himself, stunned].
Now it is all over.
[Firing, off-stage.]

ROXANE. What is it? The gunfire again!

CYRANO. Finally over
And done with. I can't ever tell her now!

ROXANE [starting to rush off].
What is happening?

CYRANO [quickly preventing her].
Nothing!
[Some CADETS enter, hiding something that they carry, and
forming a group to keep ROXANE away.]

ROXANE. But I want to know
What these men—

CYRANO [drawing her off].
Don't concern yourself. Come away.

[124]

ROXANE. What were you going to say to me?

CYRANO.   Going to say?
  Why, nothing at all.
  [*Gravely.*]   One certainty I have:
  That Christian had a brave—he has a brave
  Unmatchable spirit—

ROXANE.   Had? [*A great cry.*] Ah!
      [*She rushes among the men, scattering them.*]

CYRANO.   It's over!

ROXANE [*seeing* CHRISTIAN *lying on the ground*].
  Christian!

LE BRET [*to* CYRANO].
          As soon as the enemy opened fire.
  [ROXANE *throws herself upon* CHRISTIAN'S *body. Renewed
  gun-fire. Clamour. Drums.*]

CARBON [*his sword raised*].
  They're attacking! At the ready!
      [*Followed by the* CADETS *he goes over the parapet.*]

ROXANE.   Christian!

CARBON'S VOICE [*off-stage*].
  Come on, come on!

ROXANE.   Christian!

CARBON.   Close formation!

ROXANE. Christian!

CARBON.   Measure . . . and load!

CHRISTIAN [*faintly*].   Roxane!
  [CYRANO *quickly whispers into* CHRISTIAN'S *ear, while*
  ROXANE *dips a piece of linen torn from his shirt into the water.*]

CYRANO. I have told her everything. And it's you she loves.
      [CHRISTIAN *closes his eyes.*]

ROXANE. What is it, my darling?

CARBON.   Draw the ramrods!

ROXANE.   He moves,

I think? He isn't dead?

CARBON. Open your charges! Kneel!

ROXANE. His cheek, Cyrano, against mine—I feel
It growing cold.

CARBON. Arms at the ready!

ROXANE. Here
Is a letter . . . it's for me!

CYRANO [aside]. My letter!

CARBON. Fire!
[Musketry. Cries. The noise of battle.]

CYRANO [trying to disengage his hand which ROXANE is holding as
she kneels].
But, Roxane, they're fighting!

ROXANE. Don't go, not yet, don't go.
He is dead. And you are the only one who knew
What he really was. Was he not a wonderful person,
A great and marvellous man?

CYRANO [standing, bareheaded]. Yes, Roxane.

ROXANE. An incomparable poet!

CYRANO. Yes, Roxane.

ROXANE. A sublime mind?

CYRANO. Oh, yes, Roxane!

ROXANE. Profound
Of heart, too deep for men to understand,
So rare a spirit?

CYRANO [firmly]. Yes, Roxane.

ROXANE. He is dead!

CYRANO [aside, drawing his sword].
And death should come to me, since her tears are shed,
Without knowing it, for me in Christian!
[Trumpets far off. DE GUICHE comes from the parapet, bare-
headed, a wound on his forehead.]

[126]

DE GUICHE [*thunderously*].
  There's the expected signal! You heard it then—
  The trumpet! The relieving force!—hold on
  A little longer!

ROXANE.   There is blood here on the letter,
  And the marks of tears!

A VOICE [*off-stage*].   Surrender!

CADETS [*off-stage*].   No!

RAGUENEAU [*watching from the parapet*].   It's greater,
  The attack's greater!

CYRANO [*to* DE GUICHE, *showing him* ROXANE].
                  Get her away! I'm going in!

ROXANE [*kissing the letter, faintly*].
  His blood, his tears!

RAGUENEAU [*jumping from the parapet*].
                  She has fainted!

DE GUICHE [*raging at the* CADETS].   We shall win
  If you hold!

A VOICE [*off-stage*]. Lay down your arms!

CADETS [*off-stage*].   Never!

CYRANO [*to* RAGUENEAU].   Ragueneau,
  I put you in charge of her—take her to safety now!

DE GUICHE. Stand fast! If only we can gain
  Time, we'll be victors!

CYRANO.   Good!
  [*Calling to* ROXANE *as* DE GUICHE *and* RAGUENEAU *carry
  her away.*]
                  Farewell, Roxane!
  [*Tumult. Shouts.* CADETS *reappear, wounded, falling to the
  ground.* CYRANO, *rushing into battle, is stopped by* CARBON
  DE CASTEL-JALOUX, *who is streaming with blood.*]

CARBON. We're breaking! I got two thrusts from a halberdier!

[127]

CYRANO [shouting to the Gascons].
Courage! Don't waver, my cherubs!
[To CARBON, while supporting him.]
Have no fear!
I've two deaths to avenge: Christian, and my quiet mind!
[They come down. CYRANO raises the lance bearing ROXANE's handkerchief.]

CYRANO. Float, little flag, with her monogram in the wind!
[He sticks it in the ground and shouts to the CADETS.]
Close with them! Destroy them! [To the FIFER.]
Play us a tune!
[The FIFER plays. The wounded try to rise. Some CADETS, scrambling one after the other down the slope, group themselves round CYRANO and the little flag. A CADET, appearing on the crest, beaten back but still fighting, shouts.]

CADET. They're climbing the parapet! [He falls dead.]

CYRANO.   Come on, we'll soon
Give them a welcome which will catch their breath!
[The parapet is instantly lined with the ENEMY. The imperial standards are raised.]

CYRANO. Fire! [General volley.]

VOICE [in the enemy ranks]. Fire!
[A murderous counter-fire. The CADETS fall on all sides.]

A SPANISH OFFICER [uncovering].
Who are these men so in love with death?

CYRANO [declaiming among the hail of bullets].
These are the Gascony cadets
The men of de Castel-Jaloux:
Liars and layers of bets—
[He rushes forward, followed by a handful of survivors.]
These are the Gascony cadets . . .
[The rest is drowned in the noise of the battle.]

CURTAIN

[128]

ACT FIVE

Fifteen years later, in 1655. Park of the Sisters of the Holy Cross in Paris. The Nuns are walking to and fro across the fallen leaves. MOTHER MARGUERITE, SISTER MARTHA, SISTER CLAIRE, *other* SISTERS.

SISTER MARTHA [*to* MOTHER MARGUERITE].
Sister Claire looked twice in the glass, before I could stop her,
To admire the set of her cap.

MOTHER MARGUERITE [*to* SISTER CLAIRE].
       That was most improper.

SISTER CLAIRE. But Sister Martha stole a plum from the pie
This morning; I saw her.

MOTHER MARGUERITE [*to* SISTER MARTHA].
     Fie, Sister Martha, fie!

SISTER CLAIRE. Only a tiny glance!

SISTER MARTHA.   The smallest of plums!

MOTHER MARGUERITE [*severely*].
I shall have to tell M'sieu Cyrano when he comes.

SISTER CLAIRE. No! He will tease us!

SISTER MARTHA.   He'll say that the sisterhood
Is very worldly!

SISTER CLAIRE.   And greedy!

MOTHER MARGUERITE [*laughing*]. And very good!

SISTER CLAIRE. Hasn't he, Reverend Mother, been coming here
Each Saturday for the past ten years?

MOTHER MARGUERITE.   Many more,
Since his cousin, in her widow's veil, appeared

Beside our white hoods, like a blackbird
Among the convent doves—fourteen years ago.

SISTER MARTHA. He is the only one who seems to know
How to lighten the weight of sorrow on her mind.

SISTER CLAIRE. He is so funny! He teases us! And so kind.
To show how we love him we made him some marmalade!

SISTER MARTHA. But he's not a good Catholic, I'm afraid.

SISTER CLAIRE. We shall convert him!

SISTERS.   Oh, yes!

MOTHER MARGUERITE.   It will not do
My children, to press that point too much. If you
Torment him he may come less frequently.

SISTER MARTHA. But—God?

MOTHER MARGUERITE.   God knows him better than you or I.

SISTER MARTHA. But each time he comes he tells me, in his
    proud way,
'Sister, I've been eating meat on Friday!'

MOTHER MARGUERITE. He tells you that?—The last time he
    was here
He had eaten nothing for the past two days, I fear.

SISTER MARTHA. Reverend Mother!

MOTHER MARGUERITE.   He is poor.

SISTER MARTHA.   Who told you so?

MOTHER MARGUERITE. Monsieur Le Bret.

SISTER MARTHA.   Does no one help him?

MOTHER MARGUERITE.   No,
It would make him angry.
    [*At a distance* ROXANE *is seen, dressed in black with a widow's
    veil.* DE GUICHE, *imposing and looking much older, walks by
    her side.* MOTHER MARGUERITE *rises.*]

MOTHER MARGUERITE.   It's time that we went in.
A visitor's here with Madame Madeleine.

[130]

SISTER MARTHA [*quietly, to* SISTER CLAIRE].
  Is it the Duke de Grammont?

SISTER CLAIRE.   I think so, yes.

SISTER MARTHA. It's two months since he came to see her.

SISTERS.   The press
  Of business! The Court! The Camp!

SISTER CLAIRE.   A world of care!
    [*They go.* DE GUICHE *and* ROXANE *come forward in silence,
    and stop close to the embroidery frame.*]

DE GUICHE. And so here you stay, fruitlessly fair,
  Always in mourning?

ROXANE.   Always.

DE GUICHE.   As faithful as ever?

ROXANE. As ever.

DE GUICHE.   Am I forgiven?

ROXANE [*simply, glancing at the Convent cross*].
                          Since I came here.
                  [*Renewed silence.*]

DE GUICHE. Was he such a rare being?

ROXANE.   When you knew him well.

DE GUICHE. I suppose I knew him too casually to tell.
  —His last letter is still treasured in your heart?

ROXANE [*touching a chain round her neck*].
  It hangs like a crucifix here, a thing apart.

DE GUICHE. Even dead you love him?

ROXANE.   I sometimes wonder whether
  He is really dead. Our hearts seem beating together,
  And the life of his love somehow surrounding me.

DE GUICHE [*after another silence*].
  Does Cyrano come to see you?

ROXANE.   Yes, frequently.
  My old friend is my daily newspaper.
  He comes, unfailingly. They bring his chair

Out here on fine days, and I sit and wait
Doing my needlework. Then, never late
Or early, but on the clock's final sound
I hear—I needn't trouble to turn round—
The tap of his cane; and then he sits himself down
And after laughing at my eternal embroidery,
Tells me the latest gossip of the town,
And the evening passes . . .

[LE BRET *appears on the steps.*]

                                    Why here is Le Bret!
How do things go with our friend?

LE BRET.   Extremely badly.

DE GUICHE. Oh?

ROXANE [*to* DE GUICHE]. He exaggerates!

LE BRET.   No, it's only too sadly
As I predicted: loneliness . . . miseries . . .
His satires are always making new enemies.
He attacks all hypocrisy, won't keep quiet, he
Damns fake nobility and fake piety,
Fake heroes, and fake literati,
The lot!

ROXANE.   But they fear his sword. Not one of those
Wretches would dare to challenge him.

DE GUICHE [*shrugging*].   Who knows?

LE BRET. That isn't what I'm afraid of: what I fear
Is the abandonment and hunger, and the drear
Winter of the spirit. All these diminish him.
Those are the killers that will finish him.
He tightens his belt another hole each day.
His poor nose is the colour of old ivory.
A rusty black suit is all he has to put on.

DE GUICHE. Well, these things can happen to anyone.
Don't pity him too much.

LE BRET [*with a bitter smile*]. Marshal!

DE GUICHE. No,
   Don't pity him too much. He lived, you know,
   Without expediency or compromise.
   True to the freedom that he likes to prize.

LE BRET. My lord!

DE GUICHE. I have everything, he nothing; I under-
   stand.
   But I should be proud to shake him by the hand.
   Goodbye. [*He bows to* ROXANE.]

ROXANE. I'll see you on your way.
   [DE GUICHE *bows to* LE BRET *and goes with* ROXANE *towards
   the steps, then stops while she ascends.*]

DE GUICHE. I even
   Envy him something. You know, when a man's been given
   Great success in life, he feels (though he never did
   Anything, God knows, that was really bad)
   A thousand points of self-disgust, and these
   Add up to, not remorse, but a vague unease;
   And the ducal robes, as honours and power increase,
   Rustle up dead illusions and regrets,
   In the way that now, as you slowly walk, your skirts
   Fret the dead leaves.

ROXANE [*ironically*]. Obiter dictum.

DE GUICHE. Maybe.
   [*Suddenly, as he is going.*]
   Monsieur Le Bret, one moment! [*To* ROXANE.]
   You'll pardon me?
   [*He goes to* LE BRET *and says quietly.*]
   It's true that nobody dares attack your friend,
   But plenty hate him. Today I had to attend
   At Court, and someone said 'This fellow'—he meant
   Cyrano—'will die of an accident.'

LE BRET. Ah?

DE GUICHE. Tell him to be careful.

[133]

LE BRET [*raising his arms to heaven*].   Careful? Cyrano?
  He'll be here soon. I'll warn him, but a cock must crow!

ROXANE [*to a* NUN *who has entered*].
  What is it?

NUN.   Ragueneau, Madame, has asked if he
  Can see you?

ROXANE.   Bring him.
    [*To* LE BRET *and* DE GUICHE.] He's after sympathy.
  Since being a pastrycook-poet, he has run the gamut
  Of being a baritone—

LE BRET.   A bath attendant—

ROXANE. Actor—

LE BRET.   Hairdresser—

ROXANE.   Viol-da-gamba master.
  I wonder what occupation's the new disaster?

RAGUENEAU [*entering precipitately*].
  Ah! Madame! [*He sees* LE BRET.] Monsieur!

ROXANE [*smiling*].   Tell your troubles to Le Bret.
  I'll join you. [*She goes out with* DE GUICHE.]

RAGUENEAU [*to* LE BRET].
            Thank goodness you're here today!
  I can tell you what I dreaded saying to her—
  I'd set off to visit your friend, and was almost there,
  When I saw him leaving his house—and so I ran
  After him. He was turning the corner, and then—
  Out of the window he was passing under
  A working-man (was it by chance?—I wonder!)
  Dropped a great log of wood*—

LE BRET.   The cowards! Oh,
  God!

RAGUENEAU. I reached him and saw—

LE BRET.   Ah, Cyrano!

RAGUENEAU. Our friend, Monsieur, our poet, lying there
  With a great wound in his head—I was in despair!

[134]

LE BRET. Not dead, Ragueneau?

RAGUENEAU.   No, not—not dead.
  I carried him home (that hovel!) and put him to bed.

LE BRET. Is he in pain?

RAGUENEAU.   Unconscious.

LE BRET.   A doctor?

RAGUENEAU.   Yes,
  One came.

LE BRET.   Poor Cyrano! Roxane mustn't hear of this
  Too suddenly. What did the doctor say?

RAGUENEAU. He said there was high fever—and it may
  Mean that the skull—I hardly know what he said!
  We ought to hurry! There's no one beside his bed.
  He may die if he tries to get up, I'm convinced he may!

LE BRET. We'll go through the Chapel! That's the shortest
      way!

    [ROXANE *enters and sees them disappearing down the cloister
    leading to the Chapel door.*]

ROXANE [*calling after them*].
  Monsieur Le Bret! [*They run off without answering.*]
                    Not stopping when I called him?
  Now what tale of woe has Ragueneau told him?
                    [*She goes to her embroidery frame.*]
  The last day of September—how lovely it is.
  Better company than April's asperities.
  To sit with sorrow, smiling.
    [*Two* NUNS *bring from the house a chair and set it down under
    the tree.*]
                              An old chair
  For an old friend.

SISTER MARTHA.   The best one!

ROXANE.   Thank you, sister.
              [*The* NUNS *leave.*]
  He will soon be here. [*The clock striking the hour.*]

[135]

There! the bell sounding—
My blue skein?—It dies away. Astounding
If, for the first time, he should now be late—
My thimble?—Perhaps the sister at the gate—
Ah, here it is!—is trying to save his soul.

[*A pause.*]

She's very persevering. Impossible
He won't be coming. Nothing would hold him back—
My scissors, now!

A NUN [*appearing on the steps*].

Monsieur de Bergerac.

ROXANE [*without turning round*].

What was I saying?

[*She embroiders.* CYRANO, *very pale, his hat pulled down over his eyes, enters. The* NUN *retires. He descends the steps slowly, finding it hard to hold himself upright, leaning heavily on his stick.*]

ROXANE.   Some of these silks have faded,
It's hard to match them.

[*To* CYRANO, *jokingly.*] Tell me, have you traded
Your punctuality for another virtue
After fourteen years?

CYRANO.   It's vexing to have hurt you
Even by a moment. But I was held up, curse it!

ROXANE. By what?

CYRANO.   A particularly ill-timed visit.

ROXANE [*absently, stitching*].

Someone troublesome?

CYRANO.   Troublesome, indeed.

ROXANE. You sent him about his business?

CYRANO.   Yes, I said
'Excuse me, but today is Saturday:
There's a very important visit I have to pay
Which can't be postponed. Come back in an hour or so.'

[136]

ROXANE. Ah, well—It won't hurt him to wait, you know.
  I shall keep you here until the sun has set.

CYRANO [gently]. I think I shall have to leave you before that.
  [He shuts his eyes and is silent for a moment. SISTER MARTHA
  crosses the stage. ROXANE beckons her over.]

ROXANE [to CYRANO].
  Here's Sister Martha to be teased!

CYRANO [quickly, opening his eyes].   Ah, yes!
            [In a big comic voice.]
  Sister Martha, come here! [She glides towards him.]
                      —Those beautiful eyes
  Cast down as always!

SISTER MARTHA [looking up and smiling].
                  Yes, monsieur, but—
            [She notices his appearance, shocked.]
                                Oh!

CYRANO [indicating ROXANE].
  Hush, it's nothing! [Then loudly, boastful.] Yesterday—

SISTER MARTHA.   I know.
  You ate meat again. [Aside.] And he looks so hungry and ill!
            [Quickly, sotto voce.]
  Come to the refectory in a little while,
  I'll have some hot soup ready. Promise you will.

CYRANO. Yes, yes.

SISTER MARTHA.   You're being a little more reasonable
  Today!

ROXANE [aware of the whispering].
            Is she trying to convert you?

SISTER MARTHA.   I hardly dare!

CYRANO. It's true! Always brimful of holiness you were,
  But today I've had no sermon! It's astonishing.
            [With mock fury.]
  On my word, I'll astonish you, too!—Now let me think . . .

[137]

[*As though searching for a good joke and finding it.*]
Ah, yes! Pray for me in the chapel tonight.

ROXANE. Oh! oh!

CYRANO [*laughing*]. Sister Martha is stupefied!

SISTER MARTHA [*gently*].
I didn't wait to be given permission, I'm afraid.
[*She goes.*]

CYRANO [*returning to* ROXANE].
—Devil take me, if I ever see the end
Of your embroidering!

ROXANE. I was thinking, friend,
It was time you said so!

CYRANO. The leaves . . .

ROXANE [*looking at the trees*]. Venetian red.

CYRANO. They fall with so much courage, the brief flight
From branch to ground, knowing how to create
A last flutter of beauty, a setting-forth,
In spite of their horror of rotting in the earth.

ROXANE. Are you melancholy?

CYRANO. No, not at all.

ROXANE. Then shall we let the leaves of autumn fall,
And you can tell me all the latest news,
My dear Gazette. Are you ready to amuse?

CYRANO. Yes. On Saturday the 19th the King was ill
After eating eight large helpings of gooseberry-fool.
Two purges brought his fevered brain to reason,
And the bile was executed for high treason.
At the Queen's Ball, seven hundred and sixty-three candles
Were burned to death for bringing to light more scandals.
The rumour of a victory's getting louder.
Madame d'Athis' dog had to be given a powder . . .

ROXANE [*laughing*].
Cyrano, do be quiet!

[138]

CYRANO.   All that was Sunday:
  Nothing at all unusual happened Monday—
  Lygdamire took a different lover.

ROXANE.   Oh!

CYRANO. Tuesday, all the Court was at Fontainebleau.
  Wednesday la Montglat said 'No' to Count de Fièrly.
  Thursday: Mancini was Queen—or very nearly!
  Friday: la Montglat said 'Yes'—she's not as white as she's
    painted.
  On Saturday, the 26th—

ROXANE.   He has fainted!
  Cyrano!

CYRANO [opening his eyes, vaguely].
            What is it? What?
        [He sees ROXANE bending over him, pulls his hat further on to
        his head, and leans away from her in his chair.]
                        No, no, I'm all right,
  It's nothing.

ROXANE.   But, Cyrano—

CYRANO.   It's the old wound I got
  At Arras . . . which . . . sometimes . . . you know . . .

ROXANE.   My poor dear friend!

CYRANO. It's nothing, truthfully. It will soon mend.
                [He smiles with an effort.]
  It's gone.

ROXANE.   We all carry a wound—I, with the rest—
  Never quite healed. Mine is here at my breast:
  The writing's faded, not the stain of tears and blood.

CYRANO. May I read it? You told me once perhaps I could.

ROXANE. Oh, will you? His letter?

CYRANO.   Yes, I want to . . . today.

ROXANE [taking the silk bag from her neck].
  Here it is.

CYRANO.   May I open it?

ROXANE.   Of course you may:
Read it! [*She returns to her work.*]

CYRANO [*reading*].
                    'Roxane, farewell, I am going to die . . .'

ROXANE [*looks up, surprised*].
Aloud?

CYRANO [*reading*].
        'I think it will be this evening, and I feel
My heart so heavy with love I can't reveal,
For dying means my eyes can never again
Reflect in yours, or see when others can
The beauty I celebrated—'

ROXANE.   The way you read
His letter!

CYRANO.   '—and the movement of your head
As you brush a lock of hair away from your eyes . . .'

ROXANE. The way you read it!
            [*The darkness increases, imperceptibly.*]

CYRANO [*reading*].   'I want to give such cries:
And I cry out to you "Farewell!" '—

ROXANE.   The way
You read—

CYRANO.   '—my dearest one, my heart of day—'

ROXANE. In a voice—

CYRANO.   'My love! . . .'

ROXANE.   —a sound I already know!
[*She quietly comes behind his chair, unnoticed by him, and leans
over to look at the letter. The darkness deepens.*]

CYRANO. 'You will never be free of my love. Where I now go
There it will be, measureless, and one
With all things, always—'

ROXANE [*her hand on his shoulder*]. Cousin, the light has gone.
How can you read now?

[140]

[*He starts, turns and sees her close behind him: he gives a movement of distress and lowers his head. A pause; and then in the
dusk—the light has almost gone—she speaks slowly.*]

                         Fourteen years on end
He has played this part of being the old friend
Who comes to amuse me!

CYRANO.   Roxane!

ROXANE.   It was you all the time.

CYRANO. No, Roxane, no!

ROXANE.   Whenever you spoke my name
I should have guessed.

CYRANO.   No, it wasn't I!

ROXANE. It was you.

CYRANO.   I swear . . . !

ROXANE.   That absurd and generous lie—
The letters, they were yours . . .

CYRANO.   No!

ROXANE.   The voice was yours
That spoke in the dark!

CYRANO.   I promise—

ROXANE.   The soul was yours,
The bright spirit!

CYRANO.   I haven't loved you. It was he
Who loved you, it was Christian!

ROXANE.   You love me.

CYRANO [*his voice weaker*].
No . . .

ROXANE. Now truth has got the better of you.

CYRANO. No, no, my dearest love, I didn't love you!

ROXANE. Things that I thought were dead are born again.
Why, during all those years, were you silent, when
Here on the letter, where Christian had no place,
These tears were your tears.

[141]

CYRANO [*showing her the letter*]. This blood was his.

ROXANE. And now the silence is broken.

[LE BRET *and* RAGUENEAU *run on.*]

LE BRET.   Here he is!
I thought so! The folly of the man!

CYRANO [*smiling and sitting up*].
Naturally.

LE BRET [*to* ROXANE]. Do you know the risk he has run
To get here? He will kill himself.

ROXANE.   You mean—
Those silences—the faintness—why, were those—?

CYRANO. Ah, yes, I hadn't finished all the news.
—And on Saturday the 26th, while a lady waited,
Monsieur de Bergerac was assassinated.

[*He takes off his hat, and we see the bandaged head.*]

ROXANE. What are you saying? Cyrano! Your head!
What have they done to you?

CYRANO.   I've always said
I would die by a hero's hand at the point of a sword.
But Destiny is a mocker. She preferred
That I should be struck in ambush from behind
By a lackey with a log. It's all of a kind:
Befooled in everything, even my way of dying.

RAGUENEAU. Oh, Monsieur!

CYRANO.   Ragueneau, stop crying!

[*Holding out a hand to him.*]

What's your occupation now, my dear?

RAGUENEAU. I'm the snuffer-out of candles—for Molière.

CYRANO. Molière!

RAGUENEAU.   But tomorrow I shall leave,
I'm so mad with indignation. Would you believe?
In *Scapin* he's stolen one of your scenes!

CYRANO.   Entire?

RAGUENEAU. Yes, the famous 'What are you doing in this galère?'*

LE BRET [furious].
Stolen the scene?

CYRANO.   At least he knows what's good.
Did the scene produce the sort of effect if should?

RAGUENEAU. Ah, Monsieur, they laughed and laughed!

CYRANO.   And that's
My story, the prompter everyone forgets!
The voice in the shadow, another claims the kiss.
Ah well, the whole of my life has been like this.
And justly so. I salute, now my day has gone,
Molière the genius, Christian the handsome one.
        [The Chapel bell begins to sound. The NUNS are passing by to prayer.]

ROXANE [rising to call one of them].
Sister! Sister!

CYRANO [holding on to her hand].
                No, Roxane, don't go.
When you came back I might not be here, you know.
        [The sound of the organ being played in the Chapel.]

CYRANO. Listen—there—the music at the close.

ROXANE. Please live—I love you!

CYRANO.   No, for the story goes
When Beauty said 'I love you' to the Beast
The Prince in him was instantly released.
But, you see, I still remain just as I was. . . .
        [The moon rises.]

ROXANE. And I'm the cause of your unhappiness!

CYRANO. You? On the contrary. I've never known
A woman's sympathy that could match your own.
My mother thought it hard to call me son.
I had no sister. And as time went on
I dreaded the mockery that I should see

In the eyes of women. But you gave to me
A woman's friendship . . .

LE BRET [*pointing to the moon*]. Your other friend looks down!

CYRANO [*smiling at the moon*].
I see her.

ROXANE.   I have loved only one man
And twice have lost him!

CYRANO.   And now I find my way
Up towards the light of that moon, Le Bret.
No need to invent a method of getting there.

ROXANE. What are you saying?

CYRANO.   There, if anywhere,
Is the paradise to suit me. I shall find
More than one exiled spirit to my mind—
Socrates, Galileo and the rest!

LE BRET. No! No! It's impossible, it's too unjust!
A poet like you, a great heart, so humane,
To die like this!

CYRANO.   You're grumbling again!

LE BRET [*breaking down*].
Dear friend—

CYRANO [*half-rising, his eyes wandering*].
                    These are the Gascony cadets . . .
—The elemental mass . . . How one forgets . . .
Copernicus once said . . . Why was he there?
What the devil was he doing in that galère? . . .
          Philosopher, physician,
          Poet, duellist, musician,
          Of a heaven-exploring vision,
          Quick to throw the answer back,
          Lover, too, when all is done—
          Here lies Hercule-Savinien-
          De Cyrano de Bergerac
          Who was all things, and was none.

But I must go, forgive me; I can't delay.
The moon has come, to motion me away.
  [*He has fallen back in his chair: the sobs of* ROXANE *bring him
  back to reality: he looks at her and touches her veil.*]
Don't sorrow less for Christian, who was good
And brave and loving—but I would
Ask, when the great cold takes me, that you will
Give twofold meaning to your widow's veil
And mourning him, mourn me a little, too.

ROXANE. You know I will! I swear it, Cyrano!
  [CYRANO *shivers violently, and suddenly stands up.*]

CYRANO. Not like this! Not sitting in a chair!
              [*The others move towards him.*]
  I want no help—from anyone, do you hear?
              [*He supports himself against the tree.*]
  Only the tree.
                    [*Silence.*]
              He's coming now. Instead
Of flesh, my feet are stone, my hands are lead!
              [*He stands erect.*]
But since he is on his way here, I shall stand
Prepared to discuss the matter, sword in hand!

LE BRET. Cyrano!

ROXANE [*almost fainting*].
              Cyrano!

CYRANO.   You noseless skullhead, stare
  Out of those empty sockets, if you dare,
  Directly at my nose!—Eh? What's that?
  Resistance useless? Well, I know it, Cat!
  A man doesn't fight thinking that he'll succeed.
  The hopeless battle is the best indeed!
  —Who are these with you?—a hundred against one!
  I recognize some old enemies of mine!
  Falsehood? [*He duels with the air.*]
              Come on, then! Ha! and Compromise,

Prejudice, Corruption! [*He strikes.*] Damn your eyes,
Capitulate? Never!—And you, Stupidity!
—I know in the end you'll get the better of me:
It doesn't matter, I'll fight, I'll fight, I'll fight!
   [*He swings his sword in great circles, then stops, out of breath.*]
Yes, the last of the laurel is cut all right,
And the rose is withered. Nevertheless, tonight
When I make my sweeping bow at heaven's gate,
One thing I shall still possess, at any rate,
Unscathed, something outlasting mortal flesh,
And that is . . . [*He holds the sword aloft.*]
   [*The sword falls from his hands, he staggers and falls into the
   arms of* LE BRET *and* RAGUENEAU.]

ROXANE [*leaning over to kiss his brow*]. That . . . that is?

CYRANO [*opening his eyes and smiling at her*].   My panache.

              CURTAIN

APPENDIX
Rostand's Scene Descriptions

The scene descriptions at the beginning of each act have been abridged in the text above; here are Rostand's poetic descriptions in full.

ACT ONE
A Performance at the Hôtel de Bourgogne

The hall of the Hôtel de Bourgogne, in 1640. A sort of indoor tennis court, arranged and decorated for performances.

The hall is a long rectangle; it is seen diagonally, so that one of its sides extends from downstage right to where it makes a right angle with a stage which is seen obliquely.

There are benches running backwards on both sides of this stage. The curtain consists of two tapestries which can be drawn apart. Above the proscenium, the royal arms. Broad steps lead from the stage down to the hall. On either side of the steps, spaces for the violinists. Candles as footlights.

Two tiers of galleries along the side of the hall; the upper tier is divided into boxes. No seats at ground level, which is the actual stage of the theatre. At the back of the stalls, downstage right, a few benches are arranged in tiers; the beginning of a staircase leading to the upper galleries is visible, and beneath it a sort of sideboard decked with small candelabra, vases of flowers, crystal goblets, plates of sweetmeats, flasks, and so forth.

Upstage centre, below the boxes, the entrance to the theatre. A large door, half-open, allows the audience to enter. On the panels of the door, as well as in several corners and above the sideboard, are red playbills announcing the name of the play: *La Clorise*.

When the curtain rises, the hall is in semi-darkness and still empty. The chandeliers have been lowered to floor level, ready to be lit.

Appendix

The Poet's Bakery

The shop of Ragueneau, baker and pastrycook, a large workshop on the corner of the rue Saint-Honoré and the rue de l'Arbre-Sec; the streets, clearly visible through the glass panes of the door at the back, are grey in the first light of dawn.

Downstage left, a counter surmounted by a wrought-iron canopy, from which are hanging ducks, geese, and white peacocks. In large china vases, tall bouquets of simple flowers, in particular yellow sunflowers. Further back on the same side, an immense fireplace, in front of which, between great andirons which each support a small pot, roasts revolve and weep their fat into the dripping-pans.

Downstage right, a door. Beyond it, a staircase leading up to a small room under the eaves, its interior visible through open shutters; a table has been laid, and a small Flemish chandelier lit; it is a private room for eating and drinking. A wooden gallery running from the top of the stairs seems to lead to other similar small dining-rooms.

In the centre of the bakery, large hunks of game, hanging from an iron ring which can be raised or lowered by a rope, form a gastronomic chandelier.

In the shadows under the staircase can be seen the red glow of the ovens. Copper pots and pans sparkle. Spits turn. Pastries pile up in pyramids. Hams hang from the rafters. The morning frenzy has begun. Scared young kitchen hands, hulking chefs, diminutive scullions all jostle one another. Hats sporting cocks' plumes or wings of guinea fowl flutter everywhere. Quincunxes of brioches, villages of *petits fours* are borne on metal platters and wicker trays.

Some of the tables are groaning with cakes and cooked dishes. Others, with chairs set around them, await their diners and drinkers. A smaller table in a corner is swamped with papers. Ragueneau is sitting here writing as the curtain rises.

ACT THREE
Roxane's Kiss

A small square in the old part of the Marais. Old houses. A perspective of narrow streets. On the right, Roxane's house and its garden wall overhung with luxuriant foliage. Above the door, a window and balcony. A bench opposite the entrance.

Ivy clings to the wall, jasmine garlands the balcony, quivers and falls back.

The bench and the stones jutting out of the wall make it easy to climb up to the balcony.

Opposite, an old house in the same style, in brick and stone, with a front door. Its door-knocker is bandaged in linen like a sore thumb.

As the curtain rises, the Duenna is sitting on the bench. Roxane's window is wide open onto the balcony.

Near the Duenna stands Ragueneau, dressed in a kind of livery: he is finishing a story, wiping his eyes meanwhile.

ACT FOUR

The Gascon Cadets

The post occupied by Carbon de Castel-Jaloux's company at the siege of Arras.

In the background, an embankment crossing the entire stage. Beyond, a plain stretches to the horizon; the landscape is covered with siege-works. In the far distance, the walls of Arras and its roof-tops silhouetted against the sky.

Tents; scattered weapons; drums; and so forth. Daybreak is near. The east glows yellow. Sentries at intervals. Camp-fires.

Wrapped in their cloaks, the Gascon cadets are sleeping. Carbon de Castel-Jaloux and Le Bret keep watch. They are very pale and gaunt. In the foreground, Christian sleeps in his cape with the others, his face lit by one of the fires. Silence.

ACT FIVE

Cyrano's Gazette

Fifteen years later, in 1655. The park of the convent in Paris occupied by the Ladies of the Cross.

Huge canopy of foliage. To the left, the house; several doors open on to a terrace and a broad flight of steps. Centre-stage, a single enormous tree in a small oval clearing. Downstage right, a semi-circular stone bench set among box trees.

An avenue of chestnut trees crosses the back of the stage leading to the door of a chapel, on the right, just visible through the branches. Through the double row of chestnut trees can be seen stretches of lawn, other avenues of trees, copses, rolling parkland, the sky.

Appendix

A side-door of the chapel opens on to a colonnade covered in reddened vines which disappears, downstage right, behind the box trees.

It is autumn. The leaves above the green lawns have turned red and brown. The evergreen box and yew trees create dark patches. A carpet of yellow leaves under each tree. Dead leaves are strewn across the whole stage; they rustle underfoot in the avenues, and half cover the steps and benches.

Between the bench on the right and the tree, a large embroidery frame, with a small chair set before it. Baskets full of skeins and balls of thread. A tapestry has been started.

As the curtain rises, nuns are coming and going in the park; several of them are seated on the bench on either side of an older nun. Leaves are falling.

N. C.

[150]

EXPLANATORY NOTES

xxxi *Coquelin*: Benoît-Constant Coquelin (1841–1909), the most celebrated French comic actor of his day, known as Coquelin *aîné* (to distinguish him from his younger brother, also an actor). He performed both classical and modern comedy, and was particularly acclaimed in Molière's valet roles, as Figaro in the two Beaumarchais comedies, and as Don César de Bazan in Hugo's *Ruy Blas*. His name is above all associated with the role of Cyrano de Bergerac. The part was written for him and gave him the greatest triumph of his career; during his lifetime no other actor was permitted to play the role in Paris. Between 1897 and 1908 Coquelin gave almost a thousand performances of Cyrano, and he also performed the role in New York (1900) and in London (1901). Towards the end of his life he came often to London, where he was extremely popular. Rostand also wrote for him the lead role in *Chantecler*, but Coquelin died while the play was in rehearsal. His name lives on in the best *patisseries*: the *coquelin* is a cake made with dark chocolate and raspberries.

1 *The public arriving by degrees*: the Hôtel de Bourgogne, the oldest theatre in Paris, was situated in a wing of the palace of the Dukes of Burgundy (near Les Halles).

3 *'Clorise'*: *La Clorise*, a pastoral by Balthazar Baro (*c.*1590–1650), was given its première at the Hôtel de Bourgogne in 1631. By a harmless anachronism, Rostand sets the action in 1640, the year of the siege of Arras, which will be the subject of Act IV.

I sat up there!: this is poetic licence: Corneille's *Le Cid* received its first performance in 1636 not at the Hôtel de Bourgogne, but at the rival Théâtre du Marais.

Montfleury: a celebrated actor at the Hôtel de Bourgogne (*c.*1600–67), famous for his emphatic declamatory style and for his corpulence. The historical Cyrano satirized him in his 'Lettre contre un gros homme'.

Bellerose, Jodelet: both famous actors in the troup of the Hôtel de Bourgogne.

5 *D'Assoucy*: Charles Coypeau d'Assoucy, a burlesque author, and friend of Cyrano de Bergerac and Molière.

7 *at least a month*: the story of the challenge to Montfleury is probably apocryphal, but it dates from the seventeenth century.
   Le Bret!: a close friend of Cyrano since childhood; his 'Life of Cyrano', which prefaces the first (posthumous) edition of Cyrano's novel *L'Autre Monde* (1657), was Rostand's major source of information about Cyrano's life.

12 *The Cardinal!*: Richelieu, the chief minister of Louis XIII, was an active patron of the arts and an enthusiast for theatre.

22 *my panache!*: on the importance of this word, see the Introduction, pp. xxi–xxii.

25 *D'Artagnan*: a historical figure (1615–73), but best known in Rostand's time, and since, as one of the heroes of Dumas *père*'s novel *Les Trois Mousquetaires* (1844); both Dumas's d'Artagnan and Rostand's Cyrano take part in the siege of Arras.

49 *Pocapedious!*: these flamboyant curses reveal the speakers as Gascons. This is more than archaizing local colour, since Gascon was still spoken in the 1890s: 'In 1901 *La Semaine religieuse* of Auch lamented the passing, in Armagnac, of the Gascon-language catechism and of homilies and sermons in Gascon, which had far outnumbered those in French through the whole of the nineteenth century' (Eugen Weber, *Peasants into Frenchmen: The Modernization of Rural France, 1870–1914* (London, 1977), p. 88).

51 *Court Gazette*: the weekly *Gazette*, founded in 1631 by Théophraste Renaudot, was the first French newspaper.

54 *'Death of Agrippine'*: *La Mort d'Agrippine*, Cyrano's only tragedy, caused a scandal when it was first performed at the Hôtel de Bourgogne in 1653, on account of a line which was taken (wrongly) to be blasphemous. The play was revived for one performance in Paris in 1872.

55 *Chapter Thirteen*: Part I, chapter 8, to be exact. The idealistic hero of Cervantes's novel *Don Quixote* is an important element in Cyrano's literary make-up (see the Introduction, pp. xvii–xviii).

66 *the Tender Passion*: the 'Carte de Tendre', a characteristic product of *préciosité*, is an allegorical map which charts the three paths which lead through the land of Tenderness to love. It was invented in 1653 in the salon of Madeleine de Scudéry, and published the following year in the first volume of her novel *Clélie*. This scene satirizes pre-

ciosity, the literary and linguistic movement which flourished in the women's world of the salons and was supposed to encourage excessive linguistic refinement. The movement was at its height in the years 1653–61, but this was not the established view in Rostand's time, so the anachronism is involuntary; more importantly, Rostand's satire of the *précieuses* evokes similar satire in Molière's *Les Précieuses ridicules* (1659) and *Les Femmes savantes* (1672).

78 *changing places with* CHRISTIAN: this scene imitates a similar situation in Mozart's *Don Giovanni* (Act II, Scene ii), when Leporello changes places and clothes with Don Giovanni and then proceeds to make love to Elvira, who is on a balcony above. *Don Giovanni* was certainly in the minds of Rostand's early audiences (and of Rostand himself): in 1896, only a year before the première of *Cyrano de Bergerac*, Mozart's opera had been produced in Paris for the first time in 30 years, when it was performed in a new French translation at the Opéra-Comique. The work may have inspired the choice of subject of Rostand's last play, *La Dernière Nuit de Don Juan*, published posthumously in 1921.

91 *the virgin sky!*: the following descriptions of various means of flying to the moon are all (except for the last) taken from Cyrano's novel *L'Autre Monde ou les estats et empires de la lune*, begun in the 1640s, and published posthumously, in a heavily expurgated version, in 1657. It was often reprinted after 1855; the first full edition of the text was published only in 1909 (see also Select Bibliography, p. xxiii).

95 *the siege of Arras*: France declared war on Spain in 1635; the siege of Arras (1640) was an important episode in Richelieu's successful bid to conquer Artois. The historical Cyrano fought under Carbon de Castel-Jaloux and was obliged to retire from military life after being severely wounded at the siege of Arras.

116 *an empty stom-ach!*: in French, 'Je vais me battre à jeun!'; De Guiche pronounces the last word with the nasal twang characteristic of southern France.

134 *a great log of wood*: the historical Cyrano was the victim of just such an accident in 1654; but the legend that this was the cause of his death the following year had been disproved before Rostand's time.

143 *'What are you doing in this galère'*: the phrase 'Que diable aller faire dans la galère d'un Turc?', from Cyrano's comedy *Le Pédant joué* (Act II, Scene iv), is indeed echoed in Molière's *Les Fourberies de Scapin* (Act II,

THE WORLD'S CLASSICS

A Select List

HANS ANDERSEN: Fairy Tales
Translated by L. W. Kingsland
Introduction by Naomi Lewis
Illustrated by Vilhelm Pedersen and Lorenz Frølich

ARTHUR J. ARBERRY (Transl.): The Koran

LUDOVICO ARIOSTO: Orlando Furioso
Translated by Guido Waldman

ARISTOTLE: The Nicomachean Ethics
Translated by David Ross

JANE AUSTEN: Emma
Edited by James Kinsley and David Lodge

Northanger Abbey, Lady Susan, The Watsons,
and Sanditon
Edited by John Davie

Persuasion
Edited by John Davie

WILLIAM BECKFORD: Vathek
Edited by Roger Lonsdale

KEITH BOSLEY (Transl.): The Kalevala

CHARLOTTE BRONTË: Jane Eyre
Edited by Margaret Smith

JOHN BUNYAN: The Pilgrim's Progress
Edited by N. H. Keeble

FRANCES HODGSON BURNETT: The Secret Garden
Edited by Dennis Butts

FANNY BURNEY: Cecilia
or Memoirs of an Heiress
Edited by Peter Sabor and Margaret Anne Doody

THOMAS CARLYLE: The French Revolution
Edited by K. J. Fielding and David Sorensen